My Fantasy Dream Date With...

By H.B. Gilmour

D0963942

SCHOLASTIC INC.
New York Toronto London Auckland Sydney
Mexico City New Delhi Hong Kong

ISBN 0-590-40894-1

12 11 10 9 8 7 6 5 4 3 2 1   9/9 0 1 2 3 4/0

Printed in the U.S.A.

First Scholastic printing, January 1999

Contents

My Heart Will Go On

Alyson and Leo DiCaprio

Hi, Matt. I've got an invitation to this awesome party in Malibu and I was wondering if . . .

Alyson checked her hair in the girls' room mirror. It was frizzing as usual.

No matter how much conditioner she rinsed in or holding spray she spritzed on, humidity made her blond hair grow like killer weeds in an allergy commercial.

And today, when she needed to look extra excellent, the humidity in Los Angeles was almost as thick as the smog.

Oh, hi, Matt. Um, my sister Emma's college roomie Maggie, whose mom is, like, a major TV producer, is throwing this amazing bash over in Malibu . . .

"Ugh," Alyson grunted at her face in the mirror. She pulled the black scrunchie out of her hair and began searching her backpack for an industrial-strength barrette.

"Isn't it great living in a town where you can see the air?" her friend Serena grumbled.

Serena's hair was dark, practically black, and even more unruly than Alyson's, but she'd had the sense to rope it into a single well-behaved braid.

"Tell me about it," Alyson said, anchoring her wild mane with the barrette.

Matthew, hi! I'm going to this total rager Friday night out at the Colony, you know, Malibu, with all these kids from UCLA . . .

"I wish I was going to the party with you," Serena said, as if she were reading Alyson's mind. "I'm your best, aren't I? Your true blue? Your bud for life?"

"Definitely. But Matthew Morrison is cuter," Alyson teased, smoothing down the miniskirt she'd snagged from her big sister's closet.

She shouldn't have taken the skirt without permission. No way. But she'd needed something amazing to wear today. She *had* to get Matt to notice her.

Anyway, she'd have the choice mini back before Emma even realized it was gone.

2

She hoped.

Alyson felt an evil tug of guilt. It was Emma who had gotten her invited to the Malibu party . . . after a mere two weeks of Alyson's begging and pleading.

"Here. Are you satisfied now?" Her older sister had tossed the invitation onto Alyson's bed. "I don't know why you want to go so badly. You won't know anybody there. Half the kids are just coming to see the house anyway, and stare at Maggie's mom's famous friends."

"Of course I'll know someone," Alyson had said, impressed by the engraved card on which her name had been hand-lettered in gold ink. *Alyson Wildman and guest.* "I'll know you. You'll be there."

"Don't even think about it, Aly," Emma had warned her. "I am definitely not hangin' with you at the party. You're on your own."

"Not really," Alyson had mumbled.

And guest. That meant Matthew Morrison.

Matt was the whole entire reason Alyson had dogged Emma for the invite.

Next to Leonardo DiCaprio, whose movie posters and magazine covers papered her walls, Matt was the total most-wanted hunk on the planet. And although Alyson was only in ninth grade while Matt was a senior, she felt a sense of destiny between them.

For weeks she'd dreamed about the Malibu

beach blast. She'd had this fantasy about walking into a house full of laughing, partying, cool people with the most awesome guy of all.

Matt was that guy.

And Maggie's blowout was the perfect setting to ignite their blazing romance.

Alyson stood on her tiptoes and tried to see more of herself in the mirror over the sink.

Her sister's lemony-yellow mini looked classic, she decided. It totally went with her own tie-dyed pink-and-yellow top and new cork platforms. The outfit was as near stellar as she could pull off on a bad hair day.

"No one is *cuter* than me," Serena pouted as they stepped out of the girls' room and into the scuffed linoleum chaos of the school hall.

"There he is." Serena elbowed Alyson. "The steroidal studmuffin, himself."

Alyson looked over at the wall of lockers. Matt was standing in front of number eighty-five, the one on which, six months ago, on a dare from Serena, Alyson had actually pasted a Leonardo sticker that said, "My Heart Will Go On."

A corner of the ripped-off sticker was still visible on Matt's gunmetal-gray locker door.

"Just do it." Serena gave Alyson a little shove. "You go, girl," she whispered, then scurried away.

Alyson's face felt warm. Soon it would turn bright red. Ugh. It always happened when she got stressed out. She clutched her notebook

4

more tightly, trying to steady her suddenly damp hands.

Matt was four feet away, fooling with his combination lock.

His sun-streaked hair was pulled back in a ponytail; his brown eyes were hidden behind a pair of Bada shades. The ultra-cool diamond stud, which Serena was convinced was a Wal-Mart zircon, twinkled in his earlobe.

Matt Morrison looked every inch the hot movie star he wanted to be.

And he was alone! What were the chances of that? Only a million to one.

It was a sign, Alyson decided, knowing it was kind of dorky to believe in such things — a sign that this was meant to be, that she was right about this party being *the* place to really begin their relationship, that Matthew would say yes.

Alyson reached into the front pocket of her backpack and carefully took out the invitation. *Now's your chance*, she told herself. But her feet felt glued to the floor.

Suddenly Matt turned. He saw her. He frowned. "Yes?" he said, cocking his head at her. "You're standing there staring at my back because . . ."

"Um, because," Alyson began, "because I've got this. . . . This."

She handed him the engraved, embossed card and took a deep breath. "Matt, hi! You know my sister who used to go to this school but she's in college now? Well she's going to this amazing party over in Malibu at this awesome bungalow that'll be crawling with TV and movie people and I just thought . . ."

"You're asking me to go to a party with your sister?" he said.

"No." Alyson rolled her eyes. "She's Emma. I'm Alyson, like it says on the invitation. I mean, I was wondering if you'd like to . . . well, like it says, see, I can bring a guest. So would you, like, want to, you know, be my guest? Go with me? I mean —"

"When is it? Friday? I think I'm supposed to go to a movie or something with, like, Julie Epry or maybe it's Mariah, I'm not sure." He turned the card over in his hand. "Malibu, huh?"

"Right on the beach," Alyson said.

Matt looked up at her. He took off his shades. His warm brown eyes stared meltingly into her own wishy-washy blue-greens. "So you're Alyson?"

"Alyson Wildman." She laughed nervously. "Just like it says there." She pointed again to the invitation in his hand.

"How come I don't know you?"

Alyson shrugged. "'Cause you wear dark glasses?" That was a joke.

He didn't laugh. The bell rang. Matt handed back the invitation. "Where do you live?"

6

"Excuse me?" Alyson asked, confused.

The buff boy shot her one of his killer grins. "You want me to pick you up, right?" he said.

Yes!

It was on!

Alyson scribbled her address onto a hastily torn-out piece of notebook paper and thrust it into Matt's waiting hand, then watched as he disappeared down the hall into a crowd of fawning fans.

All she needed now was an irrestible outfit, a total makeover at the MAC counter Friday afternoon, and some way to wrestle her hair into a dynamite frizz-proof do.

"Serena, you've *got* to hit the mall with me this afternoon," Alyson begged breathlessly when they met in the cafeteria for lunch.

"Get out!" Serena squealed.

Alyson nodded her head excitedly. "He said yes! It is so happening. Pinch me!"

Serena did.

"Ouch!" Alyson shrieked, rubbing her arm. "It's an expression, Serena. You have no sense of irony. Can you go?"

"Is Leonardo buff? Definitely! Who's driving, your mom or mine?"

"I only hope the party doesn't bite," Alyson mused after school. They were on their way to the Galleria. She was sitting in the back of Serena's mother's car, wedged between a mountain of grocery bags and a smelly dog blanket.

Her platform sandals rested on a ten-pound sack of Purina, on top of which was scattered a selection of seriously slobbered-over, chewed-up dog toys.

"Why do you even care?" Serena asked. She was up front with her mother, of course, and Blackie, their cocker spaniel who, judging from the amount of hair in the backseat, should have been bald. "He said yes to *you*, not the fiesta, right?"

"Totally." Alyson forced herself to sound cheerful.

So what if she had used the bash to lure Matt? Everyone knew he wanted to be an actor. Of course he'd be into partying down with people who were in show biz or whatever.

But he would never have agreed to go with her unless he thought she was cute, or interesting, or maybe — it was possible — he, too, sensed the cosmic chemistry between them.

"Drop us at the Macy's end," Serena instructed her mom. A minute later, they piled out of the four-door kennel and into the mall.

"Ohmigod, this is so you!" Serena was shouting ten minutes later as they browsed Junior Casuals.

Alyson looked up from between two sales

racks to see her bud waving a foxy black XOXO camisole. The tiny spaghetti-strap top was trimmed with a feathery silver maribou ruff.

"That looks so fun," she said. "Not too prom night, not too clambake."

"Juuuust right!" Serena laughed.

The search for a proper skirt took exactly five minutes more.

Destiny, Alyson thought when her eyes fell on the crisp wisp of a black-and-white floral that was the same shape and length as Emma's mini — which, Alyson remembered, had to be de-dog-haired and returned to her sister's closet before it was missed.

The minute she got home, she shimmied out of Emma's skirt and ran into the kitchen to snag the Dustbuster.

She was heading up the stairs with the petite dirt-sucker in tow when her mother got home from work. "You're cleaning your room?" she said, totally amazed.

"Of course," Alyson blurted. "Mom, I am not a kid anymore. Is Emma with you?"

"She's at the library, I think," her astonished mother answered. "She'll be home for supper."

Alyson raced into her room and frantically brushed and vacuumed her sister's skirt. It was almost dinnertime when she smuggled it back next door draped over her arm, under a big bath towel.

If I pull this off without getting busted, then Matt is mine, she told herself superstitiously.

Emma's closet was color-coordinated. Alyson returned the lemony skirt to its appointed place, between Emma's favorite thrift-shop bowling shirt and an ankle-length saffron-colored granny skirt.

"Excuse me, what are you doing in my closet?"

Alyson turned around. Emma was standing in the doorway.

"Looking for a hanger?" Alyson improvised.

"For your bath towel? I don't think so. I told you, Aly, you're on your own for this party. I'm not lending you clothes. I'm not baby-sitting you through the night. Now why don't you scurry back to your messy little lair —"

"You don't have to baby-sit me," Alyson cut in. "I'm going with Matthew Morrison, my number-one dream date."

"What happened to Leonardo?" Emma teased.

"Okay, my number-two dream date," Alyson admitted. "But, Em, he is so cool. Wait till you meet him. And he's a senior. And he, like, wants to be an actor, so being at a gala with Maggie's mom's crowd will be so fun for him."

Emma laughed. "Out," she commanded. "And

show me what you're going to wear on Friday. I don't want to be embarrassed when you show up with dream boy. What are you going to do with your hair?"

"Hide it," Alyson confessed. "Being near the water is going to make it dysfunctional."

"You are such a dip," Emma said. "Your hair is great. My friends spend a fortune on volumizers, perms, and tints trying to get their hair to look like yours. And you're going to, what, wrap it into some nerd bun or wear a hat?"

"You like my hair?" Alyson was shocked.

"Hello. Yes. It's gorgeous. Wear it loose, Aly."

"Not," Alyson insisted.

That night after supper, Emma enthusiastically approved the black-and-white ensemble. "Perfect," she pronounced, after making Aly spin a third time so she could check out every aspect of the scrumptious outfit.

Then, on Friday, just before Emma left for the party, she gave two thumbs-up to the wildly tumbling blond curls that spiraled onto Alyson's shoulders, almost hiding the delicate straps of the maribou-trimmed camisole.

Matt's eyes lit up when he saw her.

"Alyson?" He checked the scrap of notebook paper on which her address was scrawled. "Whew, you look so . . . new."

11

"Thanks. I think," Alyson laughed.

"No, really," he said. "I never knew you had so much hair."

He held open the door to his Jeep, and Alyson climbed inside. On the way to Malibu, she said, "So is it true that you're serious about acting?"

"Not really," Matt admitted. "I just want to be in movies."

"Oh, doing what, directing?" she asked.

"No way. Although I wouldn't mind the big bucks." Abruptly, he changed the subject. "Mariah from school told me you were, like, in ninth grade. Is that true?"

Alyson felt herself start to flush. She turned her face away from Matt and looked out at the Palisades. "I'll be in tenth soon," she offered lamely, "like September."

"No big deal," Matt said cheerfully. "I mean, no one who'd recognize me is going to show up tonight, right?"

Alyson didn't know what to say. She knew her cheeks were getting red, and probably her neck. Soon her palms would start to sweat.

"Probably not," she told him. "It's not a high school party. It's mainly my sister's friends. They're older."

"Good," Matt said.

"So if you don't want to act, what do you want to do in movies?" Alyson tried to get back on track.

"Be a star," he said, as if that made perfect sense.

"But doesn't that mean you have to act?" she asked, confused.

"If you want to be that kind of star," he said mysteriously.

"Turn here," Alyson instructed, "where the security guards are."

She gave him the invitation, which he showed to the gatehouse guys, and they were waved through.

"Wow, look up there." Alyson pointed at the darkening sky. "There's a full moon tonight."

The brilliant circle of light was partially hidden by fast-moving clouds. The sound of the waves got louder as they approached Maggie's parents' bungalow. There was a strong, salty breeze blowing off the ocean.

It is a classic night, Alyson thought, *all clean and romantic.*

"A full moon? You think I'm a vampire?" Jarringly Matt broke the spell. "Don't worry, Buffy, I'm not going to suck your blood. Did you see that movie?"

"Isn't it a television show?" Alyson asked.

"The one with Tom Cruise. Whew. That was messed up," he said admiringly. "You think Tom will be at this bash?"

"I don't know," Alyson said, not wanting to disappoint him. "Maybe Buffy will show."

The party site was impressively immense. Matt tossed his keys to one of the valet parkers. "Don't scratch my baby, dude," he cautioned, and they trailed a line of guests through a tropical garden, past two tennis courts, and into the beach house.

The fiesta was revving up nicely. Although the glass doors at the ocean end of the cottage were wide open, the buzz of conversation and laughter and a distant, rhythmic thump of music all but drowned out the noise of the nearby surf.

Her sister had been right. Aside from Maggie and Emma, who had to be there somewhere, and a very tanned, gray-haired man in a white suit who looked familiar in a TV-announcer kind of way, there was no one she knew at the party.

Except Matt. And, at the moment, he was craning his neck, trying to look everywhere at once, as though he'd just bought an E ticket to Disneyland and was trying to figure out which ride to go on first.

"There's supposed to be a DJ here somewhere." Alyson had to shout, though they were only a few feet apart.

"Cool," Matt hollered back, without looking at her. "I'm gonna score me a cold one. You want anything?"

"Just a Coke, I guess." Alyson called, "I'll wait here for you." But he was gone.

She wondered if Emma had arrived yet. Standing on tiptoes, Alyson checked out the crowd.

She didn't see her sister or Maggie. But, after a while, with people moving past her, pushing her one way and then another, she did catch a glimpse of Matt.

He had a glass in his hand, *one* glass, and he was talking to the gray-haired guy in the white suit.

Alyson started to make her way toward them.

"I'm not interested in doing, like, the DeNiro thing," Matt was telling the man. "I see myself more as your action-hero-type phenom."

A slim woman in a silk pants suit stepped in front of Alyson. She was wearing a jangle of gold bracelets and several oversized rings. "Look at that hair. Who does you?" she demanded.

"Um, nobody," Alyson said. "I'm just experimenting with it. I mean, wearing it like this."

"Well, if you decide to cut it," the woman said, suddenly fingering Alyson's hair with her thin bejeweled fingers, "I'll buy it."

"I'm not." Alyson stepped back abruptly. "Thinking about cutting it," she explained. "Or selling it."

"Youth." The slim woman shrugged. "What do they say? It's wasted on the young."

Alison excused herself and started toward Matt again. But he was gone. The tanned man in white was talking to someone else.

Everyone, it seemed, was talking to someone else. Even the hair buyer had found a new friend.

"And who are you?" a voice demanded. Alyson whirled around. A good-looking guy with an Arnold Schwarzenegger jaw and blinding white teeth was smiling at her.

"Alyson," she said.

"Brad Barnett." He took her hand in both of his. "And what do you do, Alyson?"

"Uh, go to school," she said uncertainly.

"For what?" Brad inquired, still grinning, but a smidge less brightly.

"To learn stuff," Alyson replied, knowing somehow that it was not the winning answer.

"You mean like *school* school?" He dropped her hand.

"High school," she admitted reluctantly.

"And that's it? That's all?" He seemed so disappointed. "Great meeting you. Catch you later," he said, and vanished into the crowd.

"Are you a model?" She heard Matt's voice behind her and turned. He was leaning over a bony girl with thin, straight hair who was pressed against the wall.

Alyson didn't hear the girl's answer. "Matt, I'm over here," she called to him.

He didn't see her. But the skinny girl did. She whispered something to him, then pointed to Alyson.

Matt glanced over his shoulder and squinted

in her direction, as if he were trying to decide whether he knew her or not. Finally, he gave her this casual little wave and turned back to the maybe-model.

Alyson ducked her head, mortified. She reached into the tiny embroidered purse Emma had insisted she borrow.

She didn't know what she was looking for, really. She just needed something to do. There was a small tissue pack inside the purse. *Maybe I should blow my nose,* she thought.

"So where's the dream date?" It was Emma.

Alyson fell into her arms and gave her a fierce hug. "Oh, I'm so glad to see you," she snuffled against her sister's shoulder.

"You're smushing my blouse," Emma said, gently untangling herself. "What happened? Didn't he show up?"

"He showed," Alyson said. "He's over there . . . with a model." She turned to where Matt and that girl had been chatting a minute ago. A tiny old man in a frog-colored costume that looked like a mechanic's uniform was talking with the skinny girl. Matt had moved on again.

"Who? Not the guy in the green jumpsuit," Emma said.

"Not even," Alyson protested. "He's, like, a hundred years old."

"You said he was a senior," Emma teased.

Alyson checked the room. The glass doors leading to the deck were open. Outside, colored spotlights lit the teeming buffet table set up along one side of the pool. "There," she said. "The one with the ponytail. He's getting something to eat over near the pool. That's Matt."

Emma stared for a moment. "You're kidding," she said with a laugh.

"Excuse me?" Alyson said bluntly.

"The action hero?" Emma covered her mouth. "Oops, I'm sorry. It's just that he had Maggie's mom cornered a couple of minutes ago, laying out his blueprint for future stardom."

Alyson felt the heat rising in her cheeks again. "Am I all red?" she asked Emma.

"Kind of. Are you okay?"

"I just need some air," she decided.

Alyson pushed through the crowd and headed for the deck.

"Hey, hi. Matthew Morrison," Matt said as she brushed past him, "some blast, huh?"

Without looking at him, Alyson hurried to the far end of the deck and ran down the wide wooden stairs to the sand. She paused at the bottom, only to take off her sandals. Then, with the party noises raging behind her, Alyson ran onto the deserted beach.

The sea looked black and endless. Waves glinted and crashed out in the darkness. The sky was starless and gloomy. Despite the bright promise of the full moon, the night had become as dismal and cloudy as her heart.

A salty wind whipped her hair, frizzing and tangling it fiercely. It battered the feathery maribou trim of her camisole, which would soon look as limp and dejected as Alyson felt.

She didn't care.

Ugh. What a loser she was! Not that Matt had turned out to be a prize. He'd been so busy cruising and schmoozing and trying to promote his dumb wanna-be career that he hadn't just blown her off — he'd actually forgotten who she was!

Alyson fought back her tears. She stood in the windy blackness, eyes burning, chest heaving, as clouds blew across the night sky.

All of a sudden, Alyson realized that she wasn't alone. She could hear someone sniffling out there in the shadows. As her eyes grew accustomed to the pale light, she saw that it was a boy.

He was only a few feet away, staring dispiritedly out at the surf. His back was to her; his wind-tossed hair appeared golden in the veiled moonlight.

He was tall, slim, and seemed so vulnerable, Alyson thought. Judging by his sniffling, he was clearly as miserable as she was.

The stranger cleared his throat abruptly, surprising Alyson. She yipped involuntarily.

Startled, he whirled toward her, but the cloudy night made it impossible to really see his face.

"I didn't mean to scare you," she said apologetically.

"No, I'm sorry," he said. "I didn't know you were there."

"It's dark." Immediately Alyson felt pathetic. She added, "Like you wouldn't have noticed that without my telling you. I mean, I didn't see you, either. I just heard you . . . um . . ." She let it trail off. She didn't want to say *crying*. "What a night, huh?" Alyson gently changed the subject. "Parties can be so hard. There's always all this crushing expectation. Sometimes they're just total bummers."

"Yeah," he agreed, and started to sniffle again.

"But it's not worth getting all stressed over," she continued, determined to comfort him. "Oh, listen to me, right? Earth to Alyson. Why don't I try taking my own advice."

"Is that your name? Alyson?" he asked.

She nodded, even though he probably couldn't see her. She dug into her purse for the pack of tissues, and handed one to the unhappy boy. "You're feeling bad?"

"Rotten," he said, and blew his nose.

"Tell me about it," she murmured. "I mean, I can totally relate. Like this bash. You would not believe the fantasies I had about it. I practically broke into hives over just asking someone to go with me. And the dreams I had about him are, like, so . . . ugh. They're totally embarrassing now. I thought he was this classic babe, the king of the senior class, my dream date." Alyson winced, remembering.

"He turned out to be a loser?" the guy asked.

"Totally evil." Alyson laughed. "He blew me off the minute we got here. The boy is like on ego steroids or something. And now I owe my sister big-time. She got me invited to this gala, and how did I repay her?"

"How?" the boy asked, sounding amused.

"Oh, just by snagging one of her favorite skirts, rolling it in dog hair, and sneaking it back into her room." Alyson groaned. "Like she'll never know, right? She'll just think the Taco Bell Chihuahua exploded in her closet."

He laughed. Finally. It felt so good to hear him laugh. Actually, Alyson realized, it felt a whole lot better to make someone laugh than to try to get them to take you seriously — which was what she'd been so desperate for Matt to do.

"You know, you should probably go back inside," she cautiously suggested. "It's really a good party. I just picked the wrong guy to be with, but you'll probably have a blast."

"Are you going back in?" he asked quietly.

"Only to call a cab to take me home," Alyson replied.

She had no desire to see Matt again. Not

that she couldn't handle it. She'd *have* to on Monday.

For now, it felt good just standing out in the windy night, listening to the surf and being with a guy who needed a friend. She was so over partying.

"Tell you what, just hang with me while I put in an appearance," the boy said. "It's my friend's cousin's party and I promised him I'd show. We'll just do one lap together, then I'll give you a lift, deal? I've got to get home, too. I've got this brutal cold."

"A cold?" Alyson said. She slapped her forehead. "I thought you were crying."

"No, but I will, if you don't come back inside with me," he teased. "Man, that guy who blew you off must be the stooge of the Western world."

Alyson shrugged. "No big. He was only my number-two dream date, anyway."

"Who's your number-one?" he asked as the clouds parted again.

The moon was blazingly bright, practically turning night into day. It shone down on the boy, revealing him clearly for the first time.

Alyson gasped. "You!" she blurted, stunned beyond belief.

"*I'm* your number-one dream date?" He let out this huge cackle and ran a hand through his blond hair, trying to keep it from lashing his titanic blue eyes.

"You're . . . Leonardo DiCaprio, right?" Alyson said.

"Yup. Cold and all. Got another tissue?"

"Pinch me! I mean, don't. Not really. I mean, I said that to my best bud a couple of days ago and I'm, like, still black-and-blue."

He laughed again. "You said your name was Alyson?"

"Alyson Wildman," she said. "And I've seen everything you've ever been in."

"I don't think so," he teased. "Only about five people saw this movie I made with Sharon Stone and Gene Hackman —"

"The Quick and the Dead," Alyson hollered.

"You saw that?" He sounded really impressed.

"No," Alyson admitted sheepishly. "But I've seen *Titanic* about five times, and *What's Eating Gilbert Grape*, and *Romeo + Juliet*, and *The Man in the Iron Mask* —"

"Gee, I've got some catching up to do," he said. "I mean, I don't know that much about you." Leonardo took Alyson's hand and started walking back toward the house with her. "Like what are you interested in — besides scoring clothes out of your sister's closet?"

Alyson laughed. "Promise you won't say anything if you meet her," she begged as they climbed the steps to the deck together.

"Only if you hang with me while I cruise the bash," Leo said. "So, what interests you? You have a favorite book? You like pasta? I'm crazy about it. And peach cobbler. And Chewbacca."

"From *Star Wars*?" Alyson was psyched. "Oh, wow, he was my favorite character from that movie." People were turning to watch them. The buzz of voices grew hushed as they passed.

"Mine, too," Leonardo said. "I used to have a little Ewok village."

They moved past the pool together, past the buffet, and back into the crowded beach house, where Matt was telling the man in the frog-colored jumpsuit about his plans to become an action hero.

"Excuse me," the man said, pushing Matt out of the way. "There's Leonardo DiCaprio and his date. I've got to get their autographs for my daughter."

"Leonardo DiCaprio is here?" Matt said excitedly. "Where?"

"He's over there with the blond starlet. Is that the greatest hair you've ever seen?" the woman with the bracelets crooned. "I knew she was somebody the minute I laid eyes on her."

"Me, too," the guy with the Schwarzenegger jaw said sullenly. "I even asked her. But she blew me off with this lame story about being in high school."

"Hey!" Matt saw them. "Hey, hold up. Wait a minute. That's not his date. I'm the one who brought her here. Hey, Alyson!"

But she was telling Leonardo about being smushed in the backseat of Serena's car with Blackie's blanket and dog food and grungy toys. And Leonardo was totally cracking up at the story, laughing, and loving every word of it. So Alyson didn't hear Matt shout, "What about me? Remember me?"

But Emma did.

"Maybe when you're a superstar, she'll give you a second chance," she laughed.

Leonardo was talking about his Rottweiler, Rocky, when Alyson suddenly remembered. For weeks before she'd gotten up the nerve to ask Matt to the party, she had dreamed about the Malibu beach blast. She'd fantasized about walking into a house full of laughing, partying, cool people with the most awesome guy of them all.

Leonardo DiCaprio was that guy.

Quit Playing Games
With My Heart

Kim and Nick Carter

Kim gave up.

School was out for the day. The bicycle rack was jammed. About a hundred kids at once were pushing and shoving, trying to unlock their bikes and get them out of the rack.

Kim was holding her bike helmet in one hand and the earplugs from her Walkman in the other. The Walkman itself was stuffed into the book-crammed backpack hanging off her shoulder.

She would never be able to open her bike lock in that crowd. Her glasses were sliding down her nose. She could barely manage to keep them on.

She couldn't fix her ponytail, either. The elastic band holding it had slipped and her hair, bright red and straight as a stick, was coming loose.

Something bounced off the back of her head.

Startled, Kim turned and banged her ankle against the end of the metal bike rack.

Her so-called friend, Ben, was standing a few feet behind her, tossing balled up pieces of notebook paper at her.

"So, you going to the library or home?" he asked. Ben's voice was changing. It sounded pretty good most of the time. But every now and then, it would get thin and screechy as nails on a blackboard. His question started high and ended low.

"Home. If I can ever get my bike out of here," Kim answered, bending over to massage her scraped ankle.

Her bookbag slid off her shoulder and fell to the ground. Her science syllabus fell out, along with two Backstreet Boys tapes, which clattered noisily.

"You are such a klutz," Ben announced to the world as Kim kneeled down to gather her things.

Samantha Reese, a former Miss Junior Florida contestant, walked by with two of her devoted buds.

All three girls had long, blond-highlighted

hair and draped their bods in short, tight, neon-bright "fun" ensembles; while Kim, viciously self-conscious of her height, curves, and carrot-top, mostly hid herself in plain tees and big pants.

She was wearing baggy boxers today, with a loose tank top. The big old shirt she'd thrown over the outfit was now tied around her waist, shirttails dragging in the dirt as she scrambled to pick up her science book.

The presence of the beauty queens didn't stop Ben. "You're a walking wonk menace . . . an accident waiting to happen," he continued.

Samantha looked down at Kim the exact same way she had looked at the worms they were supposed to cut up in biology.

"Excuse me," Samantha said in her laughing voice. "She is not."

Kim was surprised that Samantha was sticking up for her. She smiled gratefully at the popular blond.

"Waiting to happen, that is," Samantha added, and gave this witchy little cackle.

One of her friends said, "Oh, please. If they had seeing-accident dogs, Kim would so qualify."

"At least they know your name," Ben said, helping her up as Samantha and her crew moved on.

"Why do they act that way?" Kim asked. "I've never done anything to them."

"Except get A's and mess with the grading curve," Ben said. "You should be proud to be a nerd. Some of the most powerful people in this country started out as simple nerds. Bill Gates. Steven Spielberg. And look at them now. Our day will come," he ranted. "Nerds of central Florida unite!"

Ben was this junior Einstein, a brainer just like Kim. He was big, plump as a butterball turkey. But he was okay with it. Ben was convinced that when he reached his full height, his weight would be properly distributed. "That is if you wind up seven feet tall," Kim would point out. She liked his weird mind and wacky sense of humor, but he could be extremely annoying.

"Will you please stop calling me a nerd," she said now.

"Oh, I'm sorry. Would you prefer wonk? Or geek? Hey, I'm your friend." He pretended to be hurt. "We geeks gotta stick together."

Kim shot him an evil look.

"Oooooh," Ben backed away with his hands raised in front of him. "When roused to rage, the shy alien turns dangerous."

"Now I'm an alien?" Kim brushed herself off and slipped one of the Backstreet cassette into her Walkman. "What's that supposed to mean?"

"That you're from another planet," Ben squeaked. "Not just you, of course. I am, too. "We're a whole other species from . . ." He switched to an exaggerated, serious news-caster's voice. "The *Popular* People."

"Maybe you are," Kim said. She switched on her Walkman, stuck in her earplugs, and returned the player to her backpack.

That fast, Ben was banished.

Like the plague, Samantha was history.

All the shouting, shoving kids around her disappeared.

And Kim was where she belonged, with Nick Carter.

I'll Never Break Your Heart, he sang to her. She could pick his voice out of the group's classic harmonies.

Nicholas Gene Carter was the youngest, blondest, tallest, and freshest of all the Backstreet Boys.

He was only thirteen when he joined the all-hottie singing group. He loved basketball, scuba-diving, his big Chevy step-side truck, Florida, and taking his boat down to the Keys. But nowhere in all his bios did it say he was hot for nerds.

Kim liked A.J., Brian, Howie, and Kevin of the Backstreet Boys, too. She thought of them as big brothers. But Nick was her secret passion.

She intended to keep it secret, too.

Ben and the rest of the science club would

never stop riding her if they found out. He could call her a space cadet, but she wasn't that out of touch.

And she wasn't lame enough to think she was the only girl who dreamed of sharing a special moment with Nick.

Someone bumped into her arm. Kim's bike helmet flew out of her hand. It skittered across the pavement, landing at the feet of the guy Samantha was supposedly crushed on, Jason Weissman, the star of Kennedy High's hockey team.

Jason looked like the stud Ben dreamed of becoming. He was a tall, slim-hipped, broad-shouldered, dark-haired, clear-eyed, clean-teethed, all-American jock, with one of those XXL jock necks about the size of Kim's waist.

Jason started to pick up her helmet. But Samantha ran over and gave it a squeamish kick with her toe. "Oooh, cooties!" she said. "It's Kim's. Don't touch it."

Then another hockey hulk booted the helmet as if it were a puck.

And a third massive jock stuck out his foot and sent Kim's headgear skidding.

"Cut it out, creep," Jason ordered.

"Play, sucker," his teammates challenged him.

With Samantha and company cheering them on, the boys kicked Kim's helmet around for a

31

while. Finally someone shouted, "Hat trick," and sailed it back to Kim.

"You'd never guess the collective IQ of that bunch is lower than room temperature," Ben said, picking up the scraped helmet and handing it back to her.

Backstreet's *Quit Playing Games* came on. Kim almost laughed aloud.

The song lyrics really went, "quit playing games *with my heart*," which was about as close to "quit playing games with my helmet" as you could get. *Pretty appropriate,* Kim thought. She could depend on the Boys to have the right song for every occasion.

The crowd at the rack had thinned out. Ben began unchaining his bike. Kim swept up her hair, tucked it into her helmet, and fastened the strap. Then she went to work on her combination lock.

Samantha, Jason, and their pals were hangin' and laughing and taking up most of the sidewalk. Kim decided to walk her bike until she got past them, out to where the street was clear.

She was inching along, holding the handlebars, when Ben came riding toward her with his hand stretched out, ready to tap her head.

Kim tried to duck, but he caught her. He rapped on the top of her helmet with his knuckles. "Hello," he sang, "anybody home?"

Then he let loose this huge donkey laugh and

gave her a thumbs-up sign, just in case any of the really cool kids had failed to notice what a close personal friend of hers he was.

"Nerd alert," someone hollered as Ben's bicycle tore by.

Behind her, Kim heard Samantha snickering.

Then her feet got all tangled up. Her bike clanged to the ground. The front wheel hit her knee as it went down.

Kim stumbled backward and wound up stepping on Samantha's foot.

"Get off my Nine Wests, geek girl," Samantha screeched and shoved her away.

"Yeah," another blond said. "Those shoes cost more than your entire outfit."

"Which," Samantha added, "was probably on the reduced rack at the Salvation Army last week."

"You mean last year," someone giggled.

Jason, the hockey jock, reached out to steady Kim.

She whirled around suddenly, surprising him, almost knocking him over.

Her Walkman flew out of her backpack, broke free of the earplug wires, and fell to the ground. The batteries and Backstreet Boys tape bounced out.

Earplugs dangling from her helmet strap, Kim stared at the smashed tape player, embarrassed and shaken.

33

"You okay?" Jason asked her.

Kim nodded yes and he knelt down to gather up the pieces of her dead Walkman. The busted machine was trailing a skinny, shiny brown ribbon of tape. "What were you listening to?" he asked, examining the wounded cassette.

"Not Yanni again," Samantha guessed, sarcastically.

"The Backstreet Boys," Kim answered Jason.

"They're my favorite group," one of Samantha's friends blurted. "Don't you love Nick?"

Samantha glared at her bud with squinched-up icy eyes.

"Well, they *are*," the girl insisted, defensively. "What's wrong with that? Everyone thinks Backstreet's the bomb."

"Hel-*lo*, we know that," Samantha said, as if she were talking to a drooler. "That is not the point."

"I think they're phat," one of the guys who'd played hockey with Kim's hat said.

"And they're from around here," Kim told him. "Their home base is Orlando."

"Oh, really?" Samantha rolled her eyes. "How new. Like everyone doesn't know that."

"The Boys are cool," Jason agreed, scooping up Kim's batteries.

Kim got down to help him. "Nick Carter's neat," she said, trying to sound casual.

"I hear his nickname is Chaos." Jason grinned at her. "No wonder you like him."

Samantha went mental over that, laughing as if Jason's remark was the funniest thing she'd ever heard.

Kim just wanted to get out of there. She leaned over quickly to pick up the tape player and banged heads with Jason. Her helmet sent him reeling backward.

"Oh gosh, I'm, like, so sorry," Kim gushed.

Samantha shrieked. "They ought to make her wear a warning label or something. That girl's more hazardous than toxic waste."

Jason grabbed his big, bony forehead and stared at Kim, speechless.

Kim dropped everything, the Walkman parts, the batteries Jason had handed her, even the torn-up, ribbon-trailing Backstreet Boys cassette.

She picked up her bike, jumped on it, and just pedaled like mad.

Her knee hurt. Her head ached. Trapped under her helmet strap, her earplugs were bouncing all over the place, banging off her chest.

The wrinkled old shirt she'd tied over her baggy boxers was flapping out behind her, flirting dangerously with the spokes of her back wheel.

She looked like a train wreck, she knew. She felt even worse.

Jason had tried to help her. And what had she done? Practically knocked him unconscious.

Clutching the handlebars, Kim sailed off the curb, tears beginning to sting her eyes.

There was a squeal of brakes. Someone, Jason she thought, shouted "Watch it!"

A horn blared. A girl screamed. Kim's bike skidded out from under her. Her glasses slid sideways on her nose and everything got cloudy.

She was soaring through the air. Then the lights went out.

Everything was dark. Kim tried to open her eyes. She had to do it very slowly. The first slit of light nearly blinded her.

She squinted, then opened her eyes to see Nick Carter's intense, blonde-haloed face staring down at her.

His brilliant blue eyes studied her face with incredible tenderness.

Kim watched him through a misty light. He looked all soft and blurry. His face would get clear for a moment, then slip out of focus.

She was lying down somewhere, and Nick was kneeling beside her. He was holding her. She was sure about that. She could feel his arms around her.

Kim blinked up at him, smiled, and wondered whether she had died and gone to heaven?

Floating above the cosmic singing star, she saw the rest of his crew.

A.J., with his earrings and peroxided hair, was wearing baggies and a DKNY sweatshirt.

All curly black hair and Latin good looks, Howie — Howard Dorough, who they called Sweet D because he cared so much about his fans — was standing next to him.

The dark-haired, green-eyed country boy, Kevin, the oldest of the Backstreet Boys, was looking at Kim with touching concern.

And Brian, Kevin's Kentucky cousin, smiled back warmly as she scanned his face.

All the Backstreet Boys were there, hovering above her like anxious angels.

"Are you okay?" Nick's voice sounded very far-away.

Kim tried to nod her head, but it hurt too much. "Am I dreaming?" she asked.

At the sound of her voice, they all smiled. Howie and A.J. exchanged high fives. Kevin and Brian beamed at her. Nick, in whose arms she rested, leaned down and planted a loud but gentle kiss on her helmet.

"Welcome back," he said, with a heart-melting grin. "You rode out in front of our limo."

"We were on our way to a recording session," Kevin said.

"Our driver hit the horn and your bike went out from under you," A.J. explained.

"You were out cold," Howie told her.

"Kevin spoke to the cops. There's an ambulance on the way," Brian reported.

Kim could feel something on her face. She wriggled her nose cautiously. Her glasses were hanging crookedly across her cheek.

"They're busted." Nick said softly. "I'm going to take them off, okay?"

Kim closed her eyes while he removed her glasses. When she opened them, Nick said, "Outstanding."

"Choice eyes," Kevin agreed. "They're green like mine."

"They're blue," Nick argued.

"Whatever," Howie said. "They got it goin' on."

"What's your name?" Brian asked.

"Kim," someone said. She thought it might have been Jason, but she couldn't see him.

Nick gently removed her helmet. Kim's long, straight hair spilled out. "Redhead," Nick said approvingly.

"Fresh," Howie agreed.

Then Jason's face floated into view. He was standing behind Kevin, trying to peer over the tall Kentucky boy's shoulder.

Nick looked up at Jason. "Is she your girl?" he asked.

Nearby, Kim could hear Samantha laugh.

"Lucky guy," A.J. said, his gold earrings flashing in the sunlight.

"Yeah, Jason wishes." It sounded like one of the jocks, but it couldn't be. They would never say anything like that.

Then someone went, "She goes to our school." And Samantha said, "She's, like, wonder-geek."

Nick looked up and frowned. "Geek?" he sounded annoyed.

"I meant that in the best possible sense," Samantha said quickly.

Kim saw Howie and A.J. exchange doubtful looks. "Yeah, right," A.J. said.

"Like someone like her would really be interested in me." This time, Kim recognized the voice. It was Jason. "She's this awesome brainer babe," he continued.

"Yeah," another guy said, "and he's just a jock."

"She'd never take a guy like me seriously," Jason agreed.

"Tough break," Nick sympathized. He tossed back his head. His chronic blonde hair glinted in the bright Florida sunlight. "She's a major babe."

Samantha gasped.

"Duh, don't tell me you never noticed," one of her friends remarked. "Samantha, you've been jealous of Kim for years."

"Slip into your Smurf nightie, girlfriend," Samantha seethed, "you must be dreaming."

"Come on, Sam. It's true," Jason said. "That's why you're always raggin' on her. Everyone knows it."

"Not even," Samantha yelped. "Okay, I am out of here! Come on," she commanded. "We are so over this."

"We?" a girl said coldly. "I don't think so."

The Backstreet Boys laughed. Nick gently brushed back a strand of hair that had blown across Kim's forehead. "How you, doin'?" he asked. "You look better than you did a little while ago."

"And that wasn't bad, considerin'," A.J. teased her.

"I never felt better in my life," Kim said honestly. Then she tried to smile, and winced with pain.

"Gangway, make room, *pardonnez moi* — that's French for move it! Let us through!"

Everyone turned toward the booming voice. The Backstreet Boys stared, dumbstruck.

Howie scratched his head. A.J. started to laugh. Kevin and Brian looked at each other and shrugged. Nick looked up. "Who is that?" he asked.

"Come on, come on, let's shake those Slim-Fast bootys." On the word *booty*, the deep voice became a high-pitched squeak. "Where is she?"

"Ben!" Kim said. This time, no matter how much it hurt, she couldn't avoid smiling.

"Brains before beauty, dudes," she heard Ben bellow. "Get out of my way!"

"You know him?" Nick asked her, staring at the hulk that had just elbowed his way past Jason and Alex to break into the Backstreet Boys' circle.

"Leader of the local wonks," Kim answered. "A notoriously annoying nerd. A dangerous geek of the Spielberg-Gates kind. His name is Ben," she said softly. "He's my best friend."

"Hey, Ben," Nick extended his hand. "I'm Nick."

"I'm thrilled," Ben said, rudely. "What did you guys do to her?"

A.J. and Howie cracked up. "Oooooh," they went. "He's baaad."

"Ben," Kim hissed. "He's Nick Carter, from the Backstreet Boys."

"That's okay," dark, dreamy Kevin said kindly. "The kid's just concerned."

"I saw Kim's bike out there. It was a mess," Ben explained. "It was all twisted up. And then I heard that she was hit by a car."

"It was a limosine," Samantha snapped at him.

"And it didn't hit her." Jason tried to reassure Ben. "Kim fell off her bike. But don't worry, she'll be okay."

A siren sounded in the distance. "It's the ambulance," Brian said. "They'll take care of Kim."

41

"The studio's been beeping us," Kevin reminded them. "We're really late. We'd better split."

Nick searched Kim's face. "I hate to leave you," he said. "Are you going to be all right?"

"Sure," she said. "Ben will take care of me."

"I will, too," Jason volunteered.

"I had CPR in my lifeguard class last summer," Samantha chimed in.

"Excellent," Ben said sarcastically. "Then you're all set for *Baywatch*."

"Okay, then. We'll see you." Nick stroked Kim's face. "You sure you have everything you want?"

"More than I ever dreamed," Kim said.

Nick took off his black jacket. He folded it and put it gently under Kim's head.

"Hey, dude." Ben stuck out his hand and helped Nick up. "Are you really from the Backstreet Boys?"

"We're all Backstreet," Nick told him, gesturing to the others.

"Prove it," Ben said.

Kim winced, and it wasn't 'cause her head hurt.

But Ben was smiling. Then Nick was, too. He turned to his group. "It'll only take a minute," he said.

"Phat," Kevin replied. "Let's do it."

Right there in the street, under the big, blue

Florida sky, without music or rehearsal, the Backstreet Boys gave the concert of their lives. They sang out in their clean harmony. They sang just for Kim.

She could pick out Nick's voice among all the fresh sounds.

"I'll never break your heart," he promised. And Kim knew that it was true.

I Don't Want To Wait

Tara and James Van Der Beek

The letter was in the mailbox when Tara got home from school. It was the one she'd been dreading, even though it wasn't addressed to her.

It might as well have been, Tara thought.

She carried the letter inside, along with a supermarket circular and the handful of bills her mom magically managed to pay each month.

Actually, there was no magic about it. Tara's mom worked two jobs to pay those bills. So, she wasn't around a lot. And when she was home, she was usually pretty wiped out.

Tara tried to help out with baby-sitting money. Her big brother, Justin, worked at the video store on weekends. And, of course, they both did all the chores around the house.

Justin really pitched in. He could do practically anything, from baking and decorating a cake — which he'd actually done for Tara's birthday three weeks ago — to fixing their mother's rusty old station wagon, which seemed to break down every other month. And he was always giving Tara and her friends rides to the movies and the mall.

Best of all, Justin was the one who listened to and loved the poems and stories Tara wrote. She had even let him read her journal once. When he got to the part where she talked about becoming a great writer, he hadn't even cracked a smile. He'd said she already was a great writer.

Tara tossed her backpack onto the living room sofa, and carried the mail into the kitchen. She set down the circular and bills, then held the fateful letter up to the light.

She knew before she did it that it was a dumb move. Like she'd really be able to read it through the envelope. Bonehead, Tara told herself. Get over it. Whatever it says is none of your business. Even if it could change your entire life.

She didn't know what to do with the letter. Should she just leave it on the kitchen table or put it in Justin's room — like in his closet, maybe, or under his bed?

Oh, that's mature. You're losing it, girl, Tara

noted. She left the letter on the table, where the mail was always left, and went back into the livingroom to tackle her math homework.

The phone rang about five minutes later. It was her mom. "Did Justin's letter come?" she asked.

"Hello, Tara, how was your day?" Tara rejoined, pointedly. "Fine, mom. And how are you?"

"Oh, gosh. I'm sorry, baby." Her mother said, "I just left DuPaul's."

DuPaul's French Cleaners was where Tara's mom worked from seven a.m. until three in the afternoon. Then she usually gobbled down the sandwich Tara had fixed for her, changed into a dress and heels, and tore across town to Ogilvey's Restaurant, where she seated people, took reservations, and worked the cash register.

"Helen got sick and I had to stay a little later than usual. So, naturally, I'm nuts. How are you?" her mother said. "Are you okay?"

"An envelope came," Tara said. "I don't know what's in it. Justin's not home yet. He's using the computers over at the library. Do you want me to open it?" she asked, hopefully.

"Yes." Her mother laughed. "But don't. Tara, we'll be all right, baby. And Justin wants this so badly. And he deserves it, doesn't he?"

"Definitely," Tara admitted.

Justin deserved a lot more than just getting into the college of his choice. He'd applied to three of them — two nearby schools, and New York University in New York City, which was the one he really wanted to go to.

The letter waiting on the kitchen table was from NYU. New York University. If it said that Justin had been accepted, then, come September, her brother would be a thousand miles away, in New York City. And Tara's life would be ruined.

She hated herself for thinking that way. It was seriously selfish, she knew. She loved Justin so much and totally wanted him to be happy. But she couldn't picture her life without him.

How would she take care of everything? It wasn't just juggling the housework and school and going shopping for what they needed, like food, clothes, all kinds of stuff. But — and this made Tara feel really evil, like majorly ill — who would listen to her? Who would pay attention to her dumb problems and tell her what to do? Who would read her reports, let alone her boring poems and stories, before she took them to school or showed them to anyone else?

Her mom had no time and way more important things to worry about. "I've got to run," she said now. "Tell him to phone me at the restaurant."

"I will," Tara promised and hung up.

She was curled up on the sofa, doing her homework, when Justin walked in.

"I don't know how you can watch TV and study at the same time," he said.

Tara looked up from her algebra book. "It's as easy as *pi*," she said, showing him the mathematical symbol π in her textbook. "Pi, get it?"

"Cute." Justin reached over and ruffled her long, loose, chestnut hair.

"Cut it out." Tara ducked her head, found the remote, and clicked off the TV.

"Did I get any mail?" he asked.

"Just one little letter," she said casually, "from . . . let me think. Um . . . NYU."

He took off for the kitchen with Tara at his heels. "It's on the table," she told him, as if he didn't already know.

Justin picked up the envelope and held it up to the light. "It won't work," Tara told him. "I tried that already. You've got to open it."

He seemed frozen. "Go on. Open it, Justin."

It was so strange, seeing Justin all nervous. And even weirder, her telling him what to do.

Finally, he tore open the envelope and unfolded the letter. "Yes!" he said a second later. He clapped Tara's head between his big, rough hands, and planted a kiss on her forehead. "I'm in. I'm accepted."

"Yes!" Tara shouted, too, even though her nose stung with the threat of tears. She cleared her throat quickly. "So you're going to school in New York, right?" She tried to sound cheerful.

"Only if the scholarship comes through," Justin reminded her.

"Well, that's that," Tara told her friend Marty on the phone, ten minutes later. "He got into New York University. I'll never see him again."

"Sure you will," Marty said. "He'll be home for Thanksgiving, Christmas, you know."

"Wrong," Tara corrected her. "He's not going to be able to fly home just because it's a holiday. He can't afford it. He'll be all alone in New York City, and I'll be all alone here. My mom always works at the restaurant on Thanksgiving. It's one of their busiest days."

"You can eat with us," Marty offered.

"No offense, Marty, but it's not the same thing," she said. "And I'm not saying that just because your family's vegetarian."

There was a knock on Tara's door. "*Dawson Creek*'s on in five minutes," Justin called. He knew it was her favorite show. She was fully crushed on James Van Der Beek, the sensitive, blond hottie who played Dawson Leery.

Justin was a lot like Dawson. He loved movies. Even before he started working at the Video Hut, he knew everything about practically every movie that had ever been made.

It was just like Justin to remember how much she loved the show. But right now, her brother's thoughtfulness just depressed Tara. Who was

49

going to knock on her door in a couple of months to remind her that *Dawson* was on? "Gotta go, it's almost eight," she told Marty.

"*Dawson* time. See ya!" Marty felt the same way as Tara did about James. They had phoned each other right in the middle of the episode where Dawson finally kissed Joey.

Tara got through first. "He's going to do it tonight," she had predicted. "He has to. I can't wait anymore."

"James so rocks," Marty had said. "What would you give to be Katie Holmes?" Katie played Joey, who Dawson was wigged over. "And, like, go mouth to mouth with James Van Der Beek?"

"Wait. Look. This is it," Tara told her. "It's going to happen now. He's going to kiss her."

Then they both gasped.

"Oh . . . my . . . god," Marty groaned, a minute later. "I have to have him. Was that the freshest, dreamiest, most stellar kiss ever?"

"I love him," Tara murmured, as dazed as if Dawson had kissed her.

But it was Justin, not James, waiting for her in the living room. "Hey, I almost forgot," he said. "I saw this at the library." He handed her a slip of paper and, before she had a chance to read it, he said, "It's an entry form for this writing contest. It would perfect for you, Tara."

"Are you kidding?" She barely looked at the form.

"It's sponsored by *Chat*, this teen magazine," Justin continued. "There's prize money for the winner and a chance to be one of the magazine's visiting editors for a week."

"I'm not a real writer," Tara protested. "I wouldn't even know what to write about."

"Yourself," Justin said, all grinning and upbeat and still sailing on his own good news. "Write what you know about, what matters in your life."

"Sure," she said, sarcastically, "that would be thrilling. Justin, in case you haven't noticed, my life is borrrring! Who'd want to read about it?"

He didn't try to argue with her. He just laughed and said he was going over to Sean's house. Sean was one of Justin's best friends. A junior college just thirty minutes away was good enough for him.

But Justin wanted to study film-making. As far as he was concerned, NYU, where all these big directors he loved had gone to school, was the only college for him.

"Thanks for thinking about me," Tara said, waving the pitiful little contest form at him. Justin was halfway out the door. "I'm really happy for you," she called.

How happy was she? So happy that she burst

into tears the minute she heard his wreck pull away.

Tara was tired. So wiped out that by the time *Dawson's Creek* came on she could hardly keep her eyes open. She watched through droopy lids as Katie Holmes, playing Joey, climbed the ladder to his room.

Everyone said that Tara looked like Joey, especially when she wore her long dark hair loose. Now, as she drifted off right there on the sofa, with the contest form smushed up in her hand, she had this dream that she *was* Joey.

In the dream, she and James were hangin' in his room and talking. Only the blond babe was playing himself, not Dawson. And he was calling her Tara, not Joey. Tara started to tell him about the writing contest. And James was all, "Excellent. Go for it, Tara."

Then they were down at the harbor. They were sitting side by side, swinging their legs over the edge of the dock.

She must have told him that she didn't have a clue about what to write. Because James started to tell her this story about how, when he was in high school, a neighborhood guy used to bully him. Then later, when James had to play a bully in a movie, he kind of imitated that guy and did this great job with the role.

"See, you can use your own life, your own experiences," James advised, "even the things that bug you out, that make you sad, frightened, or furious. You can use them for your own good."

"That is so cool," Tara said. "It's, like, if you get a lemon, make lemonade, right?"

"Wow, that's it exactly." James was impressed.

The harbor had become a kind of hiding place, with creepy moss hanging down behind them. But Tara wasn't afraid, because James was there with her, sitting close beside her.

"You're pretty quick, Tara. I never realized how really smart you are," he whispered. "I love listening to you." Then he put his hand under Tara's chin and turned her face up to his. "And you're not just bright," he added, tenderly, as she closed her eyes, and got ready for his kiss, "you're beautiful, Tara."

At that moment, of course, she woke up.

Which severely bummed her for about a minute.

As the details of her dream faded, Tara realized that James' advice was the same as Justin's. Write what you know. Write about yourself.

Well, right now, her self was all three things that James had mentioned — sad, frightened, and furious — about losing Justin. So Tara decided she'd write about a girl whose only brother is going away to college and leaving her behind.

Between schoolwork and chores, it took her two and a half weeks to finish the story. In three more, Justin would be graduating from high school. A few months after that — if he ever got the dumb scholarship — he'd be gone.

He hadn't heard from NYU again. But everyone, including his guidance counselor, was telling him to be patient, that with his grades and extra-curricular activities and the letters of recommendation he'd gotten, it was a sure thing.

"This is the best story you've ever written," Justin said, when Tara finally got up the nerve to show it to him. Even though she had named her heroine Kristy and the brother Kevin, she was certain Justin would know that it was really a story about them.

But he didn't say one word about that. He called her story awesome, really moving, intense, and excellent. He said he was proud of her. In fact, it seemed to Tara, Justin was more convinced that she'd win the writing contest than that he'd get his scholarship.

Which felt kind of weird. For as long as she could remember, Justin was always the one telling Tara that things would turn out okay. Now she found herself trying to psych him up.

"How right was I?" she got to gloat a couple of weeks later.

The letter from NYU's Financial Aid department arrived. Justin read it, then threw it into the air. "I got it. Full scholarship. I'm going!" He grabbed Tara and started whirling her around the kitchen.

The best part was that she was genuinely glad for him. Ecstatic. It was such a relief to see Justin happy again. It had been icky watching her big brother moping around the house, looking all downcast.

Although Tara had to admit to herself that, secretly, just a little bit, she'd actually enjoyed bossing Justin around, buggin' him to get over himself and get a life. It had felt kind of cool being the one with the good attitude and the right answers for a change.

That didn't mean she wasn't still blue.

"Baby?" Tara's mother tapped on her door a few nights later. "Are you awake? Are you crying?"

Without waiting for an answer, her mom tiptoed into Tara's room, holding her high heels in her hand. She had just gotten home from work. She sat down at the edge of Tara's bed. "What's wrong?" she whispered.

"Nothing," Tara said, automatically. Her mom had problems of her own. It was late. She was probably wiped out. She'd been at work since seven that morning and needed some down time just to chill. She didn't need Tara to stress her out.

And then, without her permission, without wanting to or knowing that she was going to do it, Tara sat up, threw her arms around her mother's neck, and started telling her everything.

"Oh, baby. I didn't realize you felt so alone," her mom said, when Tara finally ran out of words. Her mother took a rumpled tissue out of her pocket and made Tara blow her nose into it.

The tissue smelled good. It probably had her mom's lipstick on it and now so would Tara's tear-streaked face, but she didn't care. "We'll work this out," her mom promised, while Tara hiccuped and snuffled and tried to stop crying. Her mother swore that things would change. She'd spend more time with Tara. They'd do things together, hang out, go places and, especially, her mom said, she wanted to read all of Tara's poems and stories.

Now it was Tara's turn to wait for a letter.

The summer was nearly over and she heard nothing about the contest.

The last week of August, her mom took off from work and she and Tara gave Justin a monster going-away party.

The next day, they drove him to the train station in a sudden downpour. It rained really hard. Which was so perfect. Because everyone's face was wet, even Justin's. He tried to act like his leaving was no big deal. He reached over and mussed up Tara's hair, which was all wet and ratty looking anyway. Usually, she hated when he did that. Now, she wished he'd never stop.

"Tara! Promise you'll send me your stories," he called from the window as his train chugged away.

Tara's school started two weeks later. True to her promise, her mother took time off from work to take her shopping. They loaded up on the usual stuff — skirts and jeans and one pair of new shoes, pale purple Hush Puppies, which her mom thought were not practical but extremely adorable.

"Adorable?" Tara made a face. "Mom, they're classic," she corrected her.

"Classic shoes?" Her mother shrugged. "You're the writer," she said.

"That's harsh," Tara grumbled. "I mean, please don't remind me. I can't believe I ever entered that dumb contest."

"Hey, look at this," her mother cleverly distracted her. She was holding up the coolest outfit Tara had ever seen. The top was this luscious lilac fleece sweater trimmed in a luxurious dark grey that was almost the same color as Tara's eyes. The skirt was grey, too, a shade darker, and all slim and short and slinky.

Tara could not believe her mom had chosen the outfit. It looked way more grown up than anything she had ever owned. And it was so not a school ensemble. Although, wearing it to school would be fresh beyond belief.

"Wouldn't it be great for the holidays?" her mom said. "It would look adorable with those, um, classy purple shoes you just got."

"Clas*sic*," Tara reminded her. "But, mom, it must cost a fortune."

"We could put it on layaway," her mom suggested.

Tara checked the price tags and rolled her eyes. "Yeah, we could own it in about three years. Pass."

They came home laughing and loaded down with shopping bags. Her mom picked up the mail on the way in.

"Did you subscribe to a magazine?" she asked, passing Tara a letter addressed to her. "Oh, gosh, that's it, isn't it?" her mom realized. "*Chat*. That's the magazine you sent your story to."

Heart racing, Tara dropped her packages, and tore open the letter.

"I won!" she screamed a moment later. "Mom, it's true. It can't be true! I won! My story won first prize!"

Her mother screamed and started jumping around. "I knew it, I knew it, I knew it!" she chanted as Tara rushed to the phone to call Marty.

Marty started screaming, too. "You are so the mega-babe," she hollered.

"I owe it all to Justin . . . and to James Van Der Beek," Tara said.

"Who, Dawson?" Marty was confused.

"Yeah, he was really helpful," Tara confided, only half kidding. "Very supportive."

"So what did you win?" Marty wanted to know.

"Hang on." Tara quickly reread the letter. "Money . . . a makeover . . . and —" She gasped. "An all-expense-paid trip to New York City to be one of *Chat*'s guest editors!"

"New York?! When? I mean, do you have to skip school?" Marty asked.

"The outfit!" Tara's mom, who had danced herself into the kitchen, came charging out again like her hair was on fire. "That gorgeous outfit we saw today? The lilac sweater and the gray skirt! I'm getting it for you. It'll be perfect for New York!" She reached over and rumpled Tara's hair unexpectedly.

"Mom, get a grip! Cut that out. I hate that." Tara ducked her head and covered the mouthpiece of the phone.

"What's up?" Marty demanded, when Tara got back on.

"My family is defective. It's definitely genetic," Tara decided, checking the letter again, looking for the dates she'd be going to New York. "Thanksgiving, Marty!" she reported, stunned. "I'm going to get to spend Thanksgiving with Justin!"

"Baby, are you sure?" her mother asked, still jiggling with excitement.

"That is too cool to be true," Marty responded.

"It says right here at the bottom," Tara announced to both of them, "that I'll be spending the holiday weekend in bustling, brilliant New York City, where I'll not only visit *Chat*'s glamorous Fifth Avenue offices and . . . oh, no!" Tara shrieked. "I'll be featured on the teen magazine's fun float in the nationally televised Macy's Thanksgiving Day Parade!"

"Touch you. Whew, sizzling." Marty laughed.

Justin thought she was pretty hot, too. They phoned him that night. He was thrilled that Tara had won the contest — all told-you-so and teasing — and even happier that he'd be seeing her in just couple of months.

"You're not going to travel in your new clothes and that's final," her mom insisted as Tara packed for the journey. "It's a four hour plane trip. Just put on some slacks."

"I'm not sitting in the first class section in a pair of tacky pants, Mom." Tara tucked her cosmetic bag into the suitcase.

"The skirt will get wrinkled," her mother argued. "And what if you spill food on the top? It's fleece. It'll be ruined."

"And what if the plane crashes into a lake?" Tara asked." Do you think the skirt will shrink?"

"Don't be morbid," her mother said, but she could hardly hide her smile.

"Okay, I'll wear a life jacket when they serve dinner," Tara kidded her.

"Oh, do whatever you want." Her mother gave in with a laugh. "It's your trip. You won it. Now just have fun."

They had to take a train and then a cab to the airport.

The redheaded agent at the check-in counter told them that their plane had just arrived from Los Angeles. She studied Tara for a moment, then said, "Choice outfit. Where'd you snag it?"

Tara looked amazing. It wasn't just the ticket agent who thought so. Tara could see it herself in the full length mirror in the ladies' lounge, and in her mom's proud eyes as they waited at the boarding area.

The fleece sweater was softer than cashmere. The lilac color did something magical to Tara's face. It made her features appear delicate and pale, except for her startling gray eyes. They were no longer just big but now dark and exotic, as was her gleaming chestnut hair that tumbled onto her shoulders.

Her short, gray skirt was lined in silk. It felt dreamy against her slender legs and somehow made her feel and even look taller.

But her Hush Puppies were the best part. Funky pale purple suede with stacked gum soles, they were all flipped out and frivolous and wildly stylish.

When she stepped onto the plane, even the guy who took her boarding pass gave her a thumbs-up sign. "Third row on the far side, aisle seat," he said, grinning suddenly. Then he winked at her, and added, "Lucky girl."

Gratefully, she smiled at him, and walked to her seat.

She should have known right then what he'd meant.

A broad-shouldered, blonde guy in a blue crewneck and brown corduroys was staring out the window in the seat next to hers.

Tara said, "Hi," and started to put her backpack in the overhead rack.

"Hey, let me get that for you," her seatmate offered, starting to slide into the aisle to help her.

"Thanks, I'm okay," Tara insisted, totally focused on the crammed bag, stretching to shove it into the overhead.

But something caught her attention. The guy's voice. A blurred image of a familiar smile. The wavy blonde hair. Crinkly blue eyes.

Tara stopped and looked at him.

"Dawson?" she whispered.

"James," he said, coming out into the aisle to help her.

It was James Van Der Beek! She was going to

be sitting beside James Van Der Beek all the way to New York City.

"James Van Der Beek," she it said aloud. "I mean, I knew that. Your name, I mean." Tara shook her head at herself, as he took the bag from her. At six feet tall, he had no problem tucking her backpack away.

Dazed and grinning, she stood in the aisle watching him. Then she went, "Oops, I forgot."

James looked over at her. "You need something from the bag?"

"My journal," Tara admitted.

A flight attendant, with perfect makeup and blonde hair so flawlessly neat it looked laminated, tapped James's classic back. "Kin y'all clear the aahl?" she asked in a syrupy Southern accent.

"Oh, sure, sorry," James said. "Can you wait till after takeoff?" he asked Tara.

"Not a problem," she assured him, and they scrambled into their seats.

"You keep a journal?" James asked as they buckled their seatbelts.

Tara shrugged shyly. "I love to write."

"Me, too," he said. "I majored in English at college."

"Get out. I didn't even know you went to college," she blurted like a bonehead. "I mean, Dawson's only fifteen."

63

James gave her this funny look.

"I know." Tara laughed. "That's Dawson. You're James."

"And you're . . . ?"

"I'm Tara," she said.

"Cool." James held out his hand.

Tara just stared at it for a moment. Then she woke up and went, "Oh!" and, finally, got up the nerve to take and shake his hand.

"Nice to meet you, Tara," James said. "Have we met before? You look familiar."

"Um, my friends think I look like Joey." *She was holding James Van Der Beek's hand.* "I mean, Katie Holmes, who plays Joey."

"Yeah," he said, gently taking back his hand, as the overhead lights blinked and the jet engines revved, and the plane began taxiing along the runway. "You do, a little."

There was a phone built into the headboard of the seat in front of her. Tara wished she could call Marty, not that her friend would believe her. And then she thought about Justin. He'd be at the airport. He'd see her getting off the plane with James!

She hoped he'd have a camera. He had to have one. He was going to school to study film-making, wasn't he? Kids who wanted to make movies always had cameras, at least on *Dawson's Creek* they did. So Justin would have one, Tara decided. Maybe he'd even have a camcorder.

What if the press were waiting at the airport for James? That would so rock. And they'd walk out together and, like, cameras would be flashing and camcorders would roll and microphones on long poles would get dangled in front of their faces. Everyone would be all, "Who's the babe, James? Is she your girl?"

"Kin I git y'all a drink, honey?" The blonde stewardess was leaning over Tara.

Tara was about to say she'd like a diet Coke when she realized the blonde was talking to James.

"I'm okay," he said. "Tara, what would you like?"

The flight attendant fluttered her thick lashes at Tara. "Oh, y'all know each other?" she asked, clearly surprised.

"Old friends," James said with a straight face. "Tara?"

"The usual," she said, going along with his joke.

He cracked a smile. "And that would be . . . ?" He made a gun of his fingers and took a shot at her. "Coke, right?" he guessed.

"Diet," she said, thinking: *This isn't really happening. I am not on my way to spend Thanksgiving with Justin, sitting in a first class seat, playing mind games with my total favorite TV series superstar!*

"That was good," James said to her after the

stewardess left them. "You sure you're interested in writing, not acting?"

"So sure," Tara said. "I've been writing since I was little. Poems, stories, journals. Actually, that's why I'm going to New York."

"To write?" James asked.

"Well, no. I won this story contest for *Chat* magazine. I'm going to be sort of working there over Thanksgiving. I'll be a guest editor, that's what they call it. And," Tara added, smiling, "you helped."

James looked understandably confused.

"It's kind of dumb, but I had this dream and you were in it," she explained. "I didn't know what to write about and you told me to use my own experiences and feelings."

"Did I really say that? That's great advice. How'd I get so smart?" James teased.

Tara laughed. "Actually, you told me about some kid who used to bully you and how you'd used that experience in your acting."

"That was no dream," James said, surprised. "That's true."

"Get out," Tara whispered, awestruck. "You mean it really happened to you?"

James nodded, yes. "When I was in school. This one kid used to really ride me. What else happened in that dream?"

Tara almost blurted, *you started to kiss me*. But she thought better of it. Shrugging, she changed the subject. "I can't believe I dreamed something that really happened."

The flight attendant brought Tara's Coke and a couple of bags of roasted peanuts.

"Actually, I think I talked about that guy in an interview," James remembered. And, as Tara realized that she had, indeed, read the article James was talking about, he added with a big grin, "Hey, congratulations on winning the contest."

"The best part is that I'm going to get to spend the holiday with my brother," Tara told him. "He just started college at New York University. He's a lot like you. Well, actually, he's a lot like Dawson. I mean, he's all into movies. And he's the kind of guy you can really talk to, you know, tell him your problems and stuff. For a while there, I was really flipped about his leaving. But now things have changed. Me and my mom get along much better than we did."

"I'm supposed to do an interview with *Chat* while I'm home," James said. "I'm going to see my folks, in Connecticut, for the holidays. I know how you feel. It's hard being away from your family, especially around this time of year."

"Hey," Tara said, "Maybe I'll be the one to interview you for *Chat*. Wouldn't that be fresh?"

"Definitely," James agreed. "You know what, I bet I can arrange it. That'd be really cool."

"Get out," Tara blurted. "You'd do that? I can't stand it."

"Another coincidence," he said, "I'm going to be speaking over at NYU, down at the film school. Who knows, maybe I'll meet your brother."

"You know what," Tara teased. "I bet I can arrange *that*. You two would get along great. Justin's the best." Before she knew it, she was telling James everything about Justin and their life together and how he'd convinced her to enter the contest.

"He sounds like a great guy," James said.

"He is," Tara assured him, "He is so perfect. He's only got this one annoying habit."

"Which is?" James prompted.

Tara rolled her eyes. "Messing up my hair. I mean, he only does it when he's all emotional and and doesn't know what to say. He'll just reach out and like scratch my head and mess up my hair like I was his pet dog."

James laughed. Encouraged by his laughter, Tara went off on how she was going to get a makeover at the magazine and be in the Thanksgiving Day parade, and maybe all her friends would see her on TV.

James was so easy to talk to. Too easy, Tara noticed too late. She was on her second Coke and the stewardess was serving dinner when she realized that she'd been talking almost non-stop, practically forever. It was extremely em-

68

barrassing. "Oh, wow." She winced. "I'm way over-psyched. I'm not usually like this," Tara apologized.

"Like what?" James asked.

"I mean, like, spilling my guts out about all this boring stuff to a complete stranger. Even though it is hard to think of you as a stranger, you know? Oops, there I go again."

James laughed. "I love listening to you," he said. "You must be some writer, because you're a really good storyteller."

"You love listening to me?" Tara mused. She felt like she was having one of those been-there/done-that experiences, as if she were re-membering something she couldn't really remember. *Déjà vu*, they called it.

"You okay?" James was every bit as sensitive as Dawson.

"Sure," she said. "It was just something you said. It was weird. Not what you said," she quickly assured him. "Just that it was like I knew you'd say it."

Suddenly, she remembered. *I love listening to you.* James had said that in her dream. *You're pretty quick, Tara. I never realized how really smart you are. I love listening to you.* That's what he'd said in her dream, the dream that ended just before they kissed.

"Well, here's another weird experience." James was grinning his golden grin at her. "Not only do we have *Chat* and NYU in common, but I'm also going to be in the parade this year."

Tara thumped her forehead, dramatically. "I don't believe it. That is too awesome."

They ate their dinners, and then the flight attendant brought them warm, damp cloths to clean their hands. "You know *Dawson's Creek* really is my favorite show," Tara confided. "I'm not just saying that because I'm talking to you. My friend Marty and I are, like, totally addicted."

"That's cool," James said. "Do you have a favorite episode?"

"Oh, we were buggin' during the kissing one," Tara confessed. "You know, where Dawson finally kisses Joey. He was so cute. And hot, too." Then she got all embarrassed again. "I mean, you were so cute."

"And hot?" James was teasing her.

"Of course, I know you're really not," Tara kidded him back. "I mean, I know you were just acting."

"You still want that journal?" James asked. "I've got to get a script out of my bag; I'll get your backpack down for you."

"Thanks. A script?" Tara said, unbuckling her seatbelt and scooting out into the aisle so that James could get out. "Is it a *Dawson's Creek* script or some new movie you're going to do?"

"It's a *DC.*" He pulled her backpack out of the overhead rack and handed it to her. "We're going to be shooting it down in North Carolina next week, right after the holidays."

"That is so cool," Tara said. She unzipped her bag and pulled out a pen and the beautiful new journal Justin had given her for her birthday. It was bound in rich red leather and had her name stamped into the cover in gold script.

James glanced at the book. "Now *that* is cool," he said, admiringly. "That's a serious-looking journal."

He hauled down his own backpack. It was Navy blue canvas and twice as beatup as Tara's old bag. James took out his script, returned their bags to the rack, and got back into his seat.

"I've never seen a script before," Tara peered over at the pile of paper on James's tray table.

"It's like a short play," James said, passing her the sheaf of papers. Tara leafed through the loose pages. The familiar character names were all in capital letters, centered over their lines of dialogue. JEN. JOEY. DAWSON. James had highlighted all the Dawson parts with a yellow marker.

"It's awesome," Tara whispered.

"Hey, maybe you'll write a script one day," James said as her hand absently caressed a page.

"Maybe I will," she said, laughing. "And you can star in it. And Justin can direct." She gave him back the script and opened her journal.

They sat side by side, quiet for a while, both of them engrossed in their own activities. Tara was writing about her trip, trying to capture every moment, from her mother's crushing good-bye hug to discovering that her seatmate was James Van Der Beek.

It was amazing how comfortable she felt with him. He wasn't even James Van Der Beek anymore, he was just James. Well, just blond, blue eyed, sweet-lipped, strong-jawed, chronically-adorable James.

"Tara?" His voice startled her. She quickly closed her book. "Since I helped you win the *Chat* contest, you think you might be able to help me for a minute?"

"Definitely," she said.

"Can you run some lines with me?"

"I would if I knew what that meant," she confessed.

James' honey lips stretched into a choice Dawson grin. "Okay. Here's the deal. You read the Joey part. And I'll do —"

"Let me guess," she cut in. "Dawson?"

"You got it." He laughed and passed her the script.

For an hour that seemed like an instant, Tara was Joey. It was easy to read Joey's part like she meant it. Because she did. Like Joey, she was smart, spunky, self-sufficient. . . and she definitely knew how it felt to be fully and secretly crushed on someone who seemed unattainable. Someone like Dawson. Very like Dawson.

The only thing wrong with the script was that there was no kissing scene between them. Which, of course, Tara did not mention to James when they finished going over their parts for the third time and he thanked her and collected the pages.

What had she expected? Did she really think James was going to lean toward her and lift her chin, as he had in her dream, and say, *You're pretty quick Tara* —

"You're pretty quick, Tara," James said, stunning her. "You got Joey's attitude down on the first go around."

All at once the skyscrapers of the city came into view. James scrunched back in his seat and let her look out his window. She leaned over and, suddenly, she was very near him, almost as near as she had been in her dream.

The FASTEN SEAT BELTS sign went on. The pilot was announcing their descent into Kennedy Airport.

Tara suddenly realized that in a few minutes she would be with her brother again. She could hardly wait. And right now, she didn't care whether Justin had a camera with him or not.

"It was great meeting you, James," she said,

when the plane had come to a halt and everyone started getting up to gather their belongings.

"The pleasure was mine," he insisted. "Tara, wait," he said. Then he reached over and tilted her face up toward his.

"You're going to think I'm crazy," he said, looking awesomely Dawson, with a grin that was both mischievous and deeply sincere. "Ever since you got on the plane, I've been feeling like I know you. Are you sure we haven't met before?"

More than anything, Tara wanted to phone Marty, right that minute. *Dawson is holding my face*, she wanted to tell her best friend.

Instead, she stared up into James' amazing blue eyes and answered, "Only in my dreams."

He laughed. Then he leaned forward and kissed her.

He might have been aiming for her nose or cheeks or forehead. Tara couldn't be sure. But she'd moved her head at the wrong time — or maybe it was exactly the right time — and the kiss that Dawson had practiced giving Jen landed on her lips.

It was a soft, light, warm, perfect kiss. And this time, it was real. She wasn't dreaming. She could still feel it on her lips when she opened her eyes.

James was smiling at her. He pulled the backpack off the shelf and handed it to her.

"Thanks," Tara whispered. Then she cleared her throat and, as they headed up the aisle toward the exit, she said, "So I guess this is it."

"For now," James answered. "I'll see you over at *Chat*, right?"

"And at the parade," she reminded him.

They walked off the plane laughing together. And Justin was there! Tara couldn't see him right away because of the flashbulbs going off and girls screaming, "Dawson! Dawson! We love you!"

"Who's that?" someone hollered, pointing at her. "Is she his girl?"

Suddenly, James reached over and mussed her hair. Instinctively, Tara ducked. Then they both laughed.

"Happy Thanksgiving, Tara," James said, as the security people whisked him away.

You Make Me Wanna

Lisa and Usher

"**T**rust me, girl, he'll come," Lisa assured her friend Jonelle for the third time.

Lisa was talking about her father, of course.

Ever since her parents split up two years ago, Lisa's daddy had developed this bad habit of blowing off their father-daughter quality time together.

When he did show up, he was usually late. And he'd have all these tired excuses, like, "The alarm clock didn't go off."

Lisa doubted he even had one. But he did have a fine watch that told you the time in ten different zones *and* underwater. And, Lisa knew for a fact that it had a working alarm, because

76

whenever it was time for her dad to take her home it buzzed like crazy.

Or he'd say his car broke down. Like he'd ever let anything happen to his new blue Lexus. There was as much chance of that happening as of Usher letting his washboards go flabby.

Mostly, Lisa's daddy just forgot. In the past two years, he had forgotten to pick her up from school eight different times, take her to choir practice four, show for their weekend movie date twice, get her the gold earrings he'd promised if she pulled a decent report card, which Lisa had done to the max.

"Just remember," Jonelle interrupted her thoughts, "you said you were coming over early to help me set up."

"Jonelle, it's five o'clock," Lisa reminded her best. "Your party starts at eight. I'll be there."

"*Early,*" Jonelle stressed.

"He's picking me up at six-thirty, okay?" She had told her dad she had to be at Jonelle's by six, which meant he'd probably drive up about six-thirty.

"And you're bringin' your CDs, right? It's my birthday. And I want Mase, Cleopatra, and, especially, my man, Usher. Gotta have Usher wailing at my set."

Jonelle was totally hyper. It tickled Lisa. "Get out my face, girl," she said, laughing. "I told you I'd bring them and I will."

Jonelle was crushed out on Usher. But not half as open as Lisa was to the hooked-up, hip-hop, soul-pop, skullcap-wearin' boy.

Lisa thought everything about the singer was hot to death. The way he wore his baggies, the way he sang and moved and lived clean.

He'd made something fine of himself, Lisa thought. And not just in the gym, pumping to get that perfect bod, either. Usher had grown up poor in Tennessee, without a dad, and started singing in the church choir, just like Lisa was doing — except for the four times her father forgot to take her to practice.

"Lisa," Jonelle said, like walking on eggs. "Don't go all nervous on me. But why don't you ask your mama to give you a ride to my house?"

"Because my daddy is coming at six-thirty," Lisa retorted sharply. "And anyway, my mom's . . . busy. She's got other plans."

She was definitely not going to get into it with Jonelle about just what her mother's plans were. The whole world didn't have to know how slow her mom was behaving, all stressed out most of the time and, all of a sudden, dating!

It was like one of those funny movies where the grown-up and the kid trade places. Only it wasn't funny. It was creepier than *Halloween:*

H2O, Lisa thought, having your mother, who was the one *you* were supposed to turn to for advice, suddenly start asking you ten times a minute how she looked and was her dress too long, too short, too old, too baggy.

The same woman who used to tug and braid and cornrow Lisa's hair when she was little, now hit a life crisis over whether she should go natural or use extensions on her own.

Lisa wanted to get off the phone. "I've got to get ready and get downstairs," she said.

"You gonna wait outside for your daddy?" Jonelle asked.

"My mom won't let him in the house," Lisa confessed.

"Don't tell me they're still carrying on?" Jonelle sounded all concerned.

"How'd your hair turn out?" Lisa changed the subject.

"It braided up fine." Jonelle was off again. "Girl, tonight you'll be seein' Brandy's hair on Queen Latifah's body."

"You go," Lisa cheered. "I'll see you soon."

She had hardly hung up the phone when her mother came out of the bedroom, drenched in tacky cologne.

"What do you think?" her mother asked, tugging at her skirt. "Is it too young for me?"

The question was so tired Lisa didn't know

what to say. "What happened to your turban?" she asked, trying to get out of answering. "You were all Erykah Badu yesterday."

"It's too Afrocentric for this dress," her mother said.

"The dress is okay," Lisa said. "It's just kind of . . . small."

"You sayin' it's too tight?" her mother asked anxiously.

"It's a little snug. But you've got a good figure," Lisa said quickly.

"Really?" Her mother's relieved smile was almost as annoying as her questions had been. "I feel like I've gained so much weight. But I don't really look that heavy, do I?"

"Mama, I got to go soon." Lisa scrambled off the sofa. "You look fine. Have a nice night."

"Lisa," her mother called as Lisa sprinted toward her room. "Where you going? What time will you be home?"

"I told you," Lisa reminded her. "I told you last week and again when you were asking me this morning. Tonight's Jonelle's birthday party. You remember Jonelle." She said it sarcastically. "She's my best friend. Been my best friend since fourth grade."

"Don't be disrespectful." Her mom picked up her purse and pulled out a lipstick. It was the kind with a skinny little mirror attached to the tube. "I know who Jonelle is," she said, then started inspecting her teeth in the lipstick mirror.

"How come you don't remember, then?" Lisa blurted. "Seems like I don't count anymore."

"Don't start in on me," her mother warned gently. "I'm doing the best I can. I'm working, keeping a roof over our heads, and trying to keep this house decent, too. I don't have your schedule memorized, Lisa."

"Okay, I'm sorry," Lisa said, fast.

Well, it was better than last year, she told herself. Last year her mother needed to know where she was every minute of the day and couldn't do anything or go anywhere without her. Now she just didn't care.

"Jonelle wants me to come over early and baby-sit her before the other kids show up," she patiently explained. "So that's where I'm going. To Jonelle's birthday."

Lisa hurried into her room. She picked up the stack of disks she'd promised Jonelle, then checked herself out in the mirror attached to her closet door.

She was tall and string-bean skinny, and her reddish hair was cropped down to a tight little Jada Pinkett do. Usually, she was weak as her mom about how she looked, but tonight, bumpin' was the word. She looked good in her stretchy hip-huggers, Polo T-shirt, and strappy red platforms.

"How are you getting there?" her mother hollered.

Lisa took a deep breath. "Um, I told you," she answered as evenly as she could.

"Him?" her mother asked.

Him was her father. Her mother hardly ever used his name anymore or called him *your father*.

Lisa came out of her room and nodded. "He'll be here by six. He might even be waiting downstairs now."

"When pigs fly," her mother grumbled. "Come here and give me a kiss. I'm leaving right this minute."

Lisa pecked her mom's cheek.

"Now wish me luck," her mother said.

"Sure. Why?" she asked. She should have known better. All of a sudden her mother was hugging her and telling her about some guy named Grady with whom she was going out on a blind date. Grady drove a foreign car. Grady was six foot one. Grady made a good living. . . .

Yeah, and if Grady had told her mom he was going to a birthday party, Lisa thought, her mother would have remembered. "I thought you had to go," she said.

Her mom glanced at the clock sitting on the top shelf of the entertainment center. "I sure do," she said, all excited suddenly. She grabbed her shawl, gave Lisa a final crushing hug, then stopped at the door, her fingers poised on the clasp of her purse. "You gonna need some money to get over to Jonelle's?"

"Mom," Lisa said irritably. "He'll be here!"

Her mother shrugged, blew her a kiss, and clattered down the stairs to the street.

Lisa waited until she heard a car drive up. She ran to the window. It was a rusty old Volkswagen Jetta. Not exactly the BMW her mom had probably been dreaming about. She couldn't tell if Grady had exaggerated his height, because he didn't even get out of the car to open the door for her mother.

But at least he'd shown up.

Lisa stuffed the stack of CDs and her birthday present, three bangle bracelets Jonelle had been all that about, into her bag and went downstairs to wait on the porch for her father.

She sat down on the top step and stared out at the street. The summer trees were green and full. Two houses down, Mr. Archer was mowing his lawn. The smell of cut grass on the evening breeze was dope. At six o'clock, the sky was as bright as day.

It was still completely light out at six-thirty.

Lisa heard a car coming down the street. She stood and brushed off the back of her pants. It was an old white Cadillac, not her dad's Lexus. She sat down again.

By seven, the air had cooled a lot. *I should*

83

have taken the money Mom offered me, Lisa thought. She had a couple of dollars upstairs. But not enough for a taxi to Jonelle's.

Three times she thought about running back upstairs to phone Jonelle. But each time, she let hope and shame change her mind.

The shame was for what Jonelle would say and think about Lisa's dad. But, worse, how she would feel about her best blowing her off on her birthday.

It wasn't the CDs or the bangle bracelets. Other kids were bringing disks and gifts, Lisa knew. Aisha had a phat collection of Puffy and Mary B. and Foxy Brown. Nicole would supply the reggae sounds. And everyone had Usher.

It would have been so fine grooving to "You Make Me Wanna" tonight, she thought sadly.

Jonelle wouldn't hate her for not covering the music. But she would never forgive Lisa for being nervous and slow enough to believe in her father over her friend.

The hope part, which kept her sitting outside with her butt falling asleep, was that her daddy would show up. Not that he'd just make a late appearance, but that he'd show up in all the ways that mattered. Like be her dad again.

The hope was that tonight would be special.

Lisa needed it to be. Big as she was, tall and skinny, she felt very small tonight.

She looked up at the slowly darkening sky.

She could see the first star up there, the North Star, burning bright. It was millions and millions of miles away. It made Lisa feel even smaller.

When she was little — when she belonged to a family where everyone was pretty much where they were supposed to be when they were supposed to be there — her father had shown her how to wish on that star.

"Star light, star bright." Lisa started to recite it just like her father had taught her. He wasn't the same man anymore. Everyone knew it but Lisa. And her mom was acting like aliens had sucked out her brains. "Grant me the wish I wish tonight."

What did she wish?

That someone would come along and rescue her. That everything could change just like that. That hope would beat out shame and she would get to Jonelle's and it would be infinity fun.

Girl, you are all ran through, she decided. There is no blue Lexus comin' tonight to take you to Jonelle's set. The party is on without you.

Lisa heard a car turning the corner. It was steamin' down the road, coming toward her house.

Against her better judgment, she stood up again. She straightened out her hip-huggers and toyed with her earrings, the pink crystal dewdrops Jonelle had given her for Christmas, and she squinted into the twilight, trying to see what kind of car it was.

Dawg! It was a sleek, low, iced-out set of wheels. Lisa had never seen anything like it. It was the car her mama *wished* Grady were driving. It was gleaming black and looked like it could fly.

But it was kind of creeping along. Right in front of Lisa's house, it went *putt . . . putt . . . putt,* and stopped.

She stood on the porch steps, waiting. But no one got out.

After a minute, Lisa sat back down again, with her fists jammed under her chin, and just stared at the dead Batmobile. Finally, the driver's door opened on the side away from Lisa and someone got out. It was a guy wearing a big gray sweatshirt with the hood pulled up. She couldn't make out his face.

He put his arms over the top of his car, and then laid his head down on them.

What's he going to do, Lisa wondered, *sleep out there standing up?* She was thinking she ought to go back inside. She wasn't sure if he'd noticed her sitting on the steps yet. If he hadn't, she didn't want to move and call attention to herself.

He rested his head for a little while, then he raised it and looked right at her. "What you doin' out here all by yourself?" he called from the street.

Lisa sat dead still.

"Well, what are you doing, yourself?" Lisa challenged. "I live here. My daddy's right inside, upstairs, and he's big and mean."

"Well, I'm little and nice," the stranger said, chuckling.

He walked out from behind his car. He was wearing low-riding baggies with the hooded sweatshirt.

"My Porsche ran out of gas," he explained. "I just phoned for help." He waved what she guessed was a flip phone at her. From the steps, she couldn't tell exactly. "They'll be 'round soon."

He was slim and not all that tall, boy-size. Even in a sweatshirt and baggies you could see that. His waist was all skinny, showing out between the white band of his shorts and the bottom of his sweatshirt.

As he stepped onto the sidewalk, Lisa caught sight of the big round medallion hanging off a heavy gold chain around his neck. Inside the iced-out circle of gold was something that looked like the letter *U*.

"So you just sitting out enjoying the evening?" the boy asked. He shook back the hood of his sweatshirt. His hair was covered by a skintight black cap.

"Usher?" Lisa whispered, not believing her eyes.

"That's me," he said, giving her a sweet, sideways smile. He was coming up the walk toward her. "Mind if I hang with you till my man gets here?"

Lisa scooted over to the side rail to make room for him. "Really, really, is it you?" she said, her own voice sounding suddenly like Urkel's to her.

She looked around to tell someone. Mrs. Abbott was shaking a rug out her window. Old Mr. Archer was still mowing his yard. She didn't think they would care much about Usher. "What are you doing around here?" she asked.

"Visiting with you, looks like," the hot pop star said, kickin' the ON switch to Lisa's heart. "You look kind of dressed up. Waitin' on a date?"

"Waitin' for my dad," Lisa said, rolling her eyes. "He was supposed to pick me up an hour-and-a-half ago."

How dumb was it to tell Usher that? She was sorry the second she said it. Did she have to let the whole world know what a loser she was?

"Your big, mean daddy?" Usher smiled at her. His dark, sparkling eyes crinkled up almost into slits.

"I didn't know who you were," Lisa said apologetically.

Her hands were trembling. Her heart was pounding frantically. It sounded like hip-hop to her. The beat seemed so loud that, for a second, she wondered if Usher could hear it.

"That's okay," he said. "I know I look like a regular shorty from around the way."

A regular shorty? Nuh-uh, no way. It wasn't true, Lisa wanted to tell him. There was nothing regular about him, except that he kept it so real.

A car was coming down the street. Lisa half stood without thinking. But it went speeding by. Where was her dad? Why couldn't he come driving up now and see her sitting on the front steps with Usher? She couldn't wait to get to the party and tell Jonelle and everybody what had gone down.

Usher's car ran out of gas — yes, girl, *that* Usher! — right in front of my house! And he came on up to the porch and sat with me, while I was waiting on my dad.

But her dad wasn't coming. What made her so slow? He wasn't coming. That was, as Jonelle would say, the dilly-oh, girl, the real deal. Her father had forgotten her again. Her mother couldn't keep track of the one party Lisa had been waiting for all month.

She felt like such a dog. She had no business sitting up here next to someone as famous and fine as Usher. What was a loser doing sitting right up next to the biggest winner of them all?

This is the best and worst moment of my life, Lisa thought miserably.

Had she said it aloud? She didn't think so. But Usher seemed to have heard her. He was studying her, watching her quietly. Then, without a word, he reached over and took her hand and held it in both of his.

Lisa burst into tears.

They just sat there on the steps like that for a little bit, with Usher not saying anything, just hanging onto her hand while her head was bent down and her shoulders shook and her tears fell, making big wet splotches all over the lap of her red hip-huggers.

Finally, when she was just about out of tears, Usher said, "Tell me about it."

No, Lisa thought. *I can't. It's too stupid.*

But even as she was thinking that, words started to come tumbling out of her.

She told him about the divorce and how no one had even talked to her about it. Just one day her dad had packed a suitcase and taken his dumb sports trophies and walked out the door.

When Lisa ran into the kitchen to tell her mother what was happening, her mom was all tight-lipped and didn't even turn around from the sink where she was cleaning a chicken for supper. She just gave this quick little nod of her head and said, "I know."

That was it, that was all. She knew. And he knew. And no one bothered to let Lisa know until it was too late.

Then the crying began. She'd come home from school, and her mother would be lying up in bed with the shades down in her room, crying and crying. Mom would be in her nightie from morning till night, and no supper made and no lights on in the rest of the house.

So then Lisa couldn't have anyone come over anymore. The place was a mess and her mama was a mess and it was embarrassing and scary because, back then, Lisa didn't even know how to cook and she was afraid that she and her mom would starve to death if someone didn't do something quick.

Her friend Jonelle's mama, Mrs. Green, could cook like a dog. So Lisa practically lived over there for a while. Mrs. Green would fix her covered dishes to take home for her mother. And Jonelle was so fine the whole time. She didn't ask a lot of questions or tell everybody at school what had gone down. They'd just hang like always. Only tighter. Jonelle became her best friend ever.

And tonight was Jonelle's birthday party. All she'd asked was for Lisa to get herself over there early and stay with her till the other kids arrived. Oh, and bring some sounds.

"I was supposed to bring you," Lisa said. "I mean your CDs and all. My mom had this hot date tonight so my dad was going to drop me off at Jonelle's. And everyone, Jonelle and my mother, everyone knew he wouldn't make it. Everyone but me. He hasn't showed up yet. And Jonelle must be so mad, she'll probably never speak to me again."

"I got a best named Jonetta," Usher said. He had let go of her hand and come up with a clean handkerchief, which he shook open now and gave to her. "She's my mother. My mother, my manager, and my best friend."

"Straight up?" Lisa said.

"On the real," Usher confirmed. "My daddy split, too, when I was born. That's the game, you just gotta play harder. But my mother watches my back."

"My mom's getting better," Lisa said. "She's not crying anymore. And she's got a job where she's doing good. And now she's starting to go out on dates, so she's not all over my stuff anymore."

"There you go," Usher said. "Things are lookin' up already."

Lisa wiped her face. She wanted to blow her nose, but she didn't want to mess up Usher's fresh clean hanky. So she folded it back up neatly and sat there sniffling for a while.

Usher pulled out his flip phone. "Just checkin' on my man."

"I really love your songs," Lisa said. "So does Jonelle. They're probably playing right now at the party."

"Which one gets it goin' on for you?" he asked, punching in the number.

"All of them, but especially 'You Make Me Wanna.'"

Usher laughed. Then he held up a finger and started talking to the person he'd called. Finally, he went, "A'ight," and clicked off. "He's six blocks away in the limo. Be right here. So you like 'You Make Me Wanna'?"

"It opens me," Lisa said softly.

Usher tucked his phone into his sweatshirt pocket and stood up. "Well, you know what *you* make me wanna?" he asked.

Lisa shook her head. "What?"

"You make me wanna . . . take you to the party." Usher jumped off the porch and did this kickin' twirl.

His huge gray sweatshirt flew open. His gold medallion swung and thumped on his silky bare chest. And he started moving just like in his video.

Usher was dancing on Lisa's front lawn. Dancing and singing "You Make Me Wanna," only he was changing the words. He was singing about driving Lisa over to Jonelle's party!

Before she knew it, Lisa had jumped up and started singing with him. She didn't know the new words, of course. He was making them up as he went along. So she waited till he sang a line, and then she sang it after him, in harmony.

Usher grinned at her encouragingly. "Nice and slow," he hollered once. Then he quickly spun out a new line.

She saw a couple of lights go on across the way. People started peeking out of their windows to see what was going down.

A car pulled up. Its headlights caught Usher making his moves. The driver stopped and kept his beams focused on the singer like a spotlight. And then a pickup truck came the other way down the street. It, too, stopped and aimed its brights at Usher.

Standing on the top step of her porch, rockin' and singin' out, Lisa waved at her startled neighbors. Most of them waved back. Mrs. Harris, in a second-floor bay window, was holding a white hanky in one hand and waving both her arms to the music.

Finally a long black limousine pulled up behind Usher's black Porsche Boxster. Usher did a final spin and the show was over.

People applauded from their porches and windows and cars. Two guys got out of the limo and talked with Usher for a while, then got to work on the Porsche.

"That was fine," Usher told Lisa, while the men refilled his gas tank. "Where'd you learn to sing like that?"

"Church," Lisa said. She was all flushed and warm, feeling fine.

"You sing in the choir?" Usher asked. When she nodded yes, he said, "That's where I started singing. I used to sing in the church choir back in Tennessee. My mother wanted me to go to church. That's how she kept me there."

"Are you really going to drive me over to the party?" Lisa asked.

"We're on, girl," he declared. "I'm gonna just go rap with my guys and you decide. You want to go in the limo or my Porsche?" Hurrying back to his car, he called, "Your choice."

"Lisa?"

It was past eight. It was dark out. But she saw him coming toward her under the street lamp. It was her dad. He had gotten out of one of the cars that had shone its headlights on their concert.

"Daddy?" Lisa said. She was almost as surprised to see him as she had been to see Usher climbing out of his gleaming black Boxster.

"I forgot again," he said.

"What broke down this time?" Lisa asked, trying to stay mad at him, but too glad to see him to sound convincingly cold. "The car or the clock?"

He ignored her sarcasm. "Is it too late?"

"For you to drive me over to Jonelle's? Well, yeah," she said, "Usher's going to take me by there in his Porsche."

"You'd rather go with him than me?" her Daddy asked.

"I was waiting for you," Lisa explained. "I was counting on you, Daddy. I sat out here till it got dark and I thought, for sure, I'd miss my best friend's birthday party. I was feeling really bad. Then Usher showed up, just like an angel. And, yeah, I want to go over to Jonelle's with him."

"I'm sorry," her father said. He opened his arms and she moved right into them. "Don't give up on me, okay? I'll do better."

Lisa walked him back to his Lexus and he gave her a hug and took off. "I got choir practice Tuesday!" she hollered after him.

Usher came over. "Okay, we're gassed up and ready to roll. Which car you want to take?"

"You choose," Lisa said. "I'm real tired."

Usher thought about it. "My Boxster's phat, but I think a long, black, chauffeured limousine is the way to go tonight."

Fifteen minutes later, they pulled up outside Jonelle's place. The limo was nearly as long as the house was. Lisa grabbed her backpack and climbed out.

Everyone ran outside. Jonelle was the last one through the door.

"It's Lisa," someone told her. "She drove up in that limousine."

"Your daddy win the lottery?" Jonelle asked,

all cold. "Or he just got himself a chauffeur's job?"

"You were right," Lisa said. "He was late."

"Why am I not surprised? Well, you missed a bumpin' party, girl." Jonelle was trying to punish her. "I got the coolest gifts ever." She waggled a bottle of Calvin Klein perfume at Lisa. "I am drowning in CK, CDs, and Gap T-shirts."

"Well, I got you something, Jonelle," Lisa said, trying not to smile. "You asked me to bring Usher, didn't you?"

"We *got* Usher. Aisha, Nicole, and Sukari brought Usher," Jonelle said, acting all bored.

"Nuh-uh," Lisa said. "I mean, I brought . . . Usher!"

The tinted window rolled down and there he was, giving Jonelle his crinkly-eyed, sideways grin from the back of the limo. "Happy birthday, Jonelle," Usher called out. "Lisa sure thinks you got it goin' on."

Jonelle screamed. Then she threw her arms around Lisa. "Thank you, thank you, thank you," she kept hollering. "This is my best birthday ever and you are my best for life!"

I Will Come To You

Sarah and Taylor Hanson

Sarah was desperate. She tossed down her backpack and didn't even wince when she heard the candle jar inside it clunk against the kitchen table. "You just don't get it. Hanson is going to be here for two nights only, Mom!"

Sarah had bought the bayberry-scented candle because it would look excellent under her new poster of Taylor. Now she didn't even care if it broke.

Her mother was washing lettuce at the kitchen sink. "No means no," she repeated over her shoulder. "You are not spending the night on the street, Sarah. That's final."

"That is so cold," Sarah complained. She elbowed her friend Jennifer.

"Honestly, Mrs. Mills," Jennifer took the cue. "If we're not at the Sound Shack when tickets go on sale tomorrow morning, we'll never get into the concert. Hanson is the hottest group ever."

"Handsome?" Sarah's Grandma Lily, who was visiting from New York, walked into the kitchen. She was wearing khakis — Gap khakis and a sweatshirt and leather sandals from which her bright red-painted toenails peeked. Grandma Lily's gray-streaked hair was pulled back in a ponytail. "What kind of group calls itself Handsome?" she asked, her hazel eyes sparkling with amusement.

Sarah ran to her. "Grandma Lily, you're here!"

"It's *Hanson*," Jennifer pronounced the name carefully. "They're so cute. And, like, totally talented. And they're very into family, Mrs. Mills." Jennifer went back to work on Sarah's mother.

"Especially Taylor," Sarah said, hugging her grandmother. "He's the middle brother and, Grandma, he is so fine! I've got to see him in person. They're only going to be here for two days. Please, please, please, Grandma, make her let us go."

"Sarah, stop," her grandmother said gently. "You know I can't interfere with your mother's decisions. She's your mother. She loves you. She

wouldn't do anything to hurt you, right, Anne?"
Sarah's grandmother looked over at her daughter. "You don't want them to go to this concert?" she asked mildly.

Sarah's mother stopped washing lettuce. She dried her hands on the apron she was wearing over her skirt and blouse. Sarah's mom was a lawyer and wore practically the same thing every day, dark suit, light blouse, lipstick only. "It's not the concert. She wants to stay out all night, on the street."

"It's not like that," Sarah blurted. "We just want to wait in line until tickets go on sale. The Sound Shack opens at nine and everyone will rush in and buy, like, a million tickets each. By the time we get out of school —"

"Or even if we could get over there during lunch period —" Jennifer put in sadly.

"There won't be any tickets left," Sarah finished.

Her mother and grandmother exchanged looks. Her mother's look said, *See what I have to put up with?* Her grandmother's look was, *I know, darling, but is it really so terrible?*

"What about you?" Grandma Lily turned to Jennifer. "Are your parents letting you stay out all night?"

"Only if Sarah can," Jennifer reported.

"Where is it?" her grandmother asked. "The Sound Shack, is it near here?"

100

"It's not that far away," Sarah said.

"It's downtown," her mother contradicted her. "It's a rotten neighborhood after dark."

"Yeah, but there'll be, like, hundreds of people there and probably police and everything," Sarah insisted.

"Mom," Sarah's mother interrupted, "can you give me a hand with the potatoes?"

"I'll do them," Sarah volunteered. "I'll peel the potatoes and set the table and wash the dishes and scrub the floor and clean my room and baby-sit Jeremy and, like, really help out with everything, Mom —"

"Sarah, please." Her mother sounded tired now. Not worn down and ready to give in, but just plain over it. Like if she'd had a magic wand, she'd wave it now and make Sarah disappear. "It's not just my decision," she said. "It's your father's, too. We talked it over. The answer is no."

Poof! Sarah was gone.

She grabbed her backpack and, with Jennifer scurrying behind her, stalked out of the room.

"Sarah, you have to set the table," her mother called sharply.

"It's all right, Anne. I'll do it," she heard her grandmother say. "Let her go upstairs."

Jennifer gave Sarah a hug before she left for home. "We'll get the tickets some way," she tried to comfort her.

"This is so bad." Sarah was practically in tears. "I can't believe Taylor Hanson is going to be at the stadium, like a couple of miles away, and I'm actually not going to get to see him."

"You and Tay are destiny, remember?" Jennifer urged. "Be positive."

After Jennifer left, Sarah trudged up to her room. She unpacked the bayberry mood candle in its frosted glass jar. *It isn't broken, it's only a little chipped — like my dreams,* she thought.

Sarah set the candle down on her dresser, under the poster of Taylor in his bright red tennis shirt, his long blond hair framing his golden, smiling, slightly flushed face.

Jennifer was right. Someway, somehow, Sarah would see Taylor. And when they met, sparks would fly. She would find a way. Love always found a way.

Dinner was a bummer. Sarah tried to bring up the ticket situation again.

Her mother just threw her this annoyed, tight-lipped look.

Her father said, "We've already discussed this, Sarah. Pass the potatoes, please. Enough."

Her nine-year-old brother, Jeremy, added for good measure, "Hanson blows."

Only Grandma Lily seemed sympathetic, for all that was worth. After dinner, she came up to Sarah's bedroom. "Smells wonderful in here," she said, noting the candles Sarah had lit. "Very pretty. Is he the one?" she asked, studying a poster of Taylor in concert, wearing a black leather jacket over a black T-shirt, with all his cool beaded chokers and charms.

Sarah said it was — Jordan Taylor Hanson, who everyone called Taylor or sometimes Tay. He was amazingly talented and artistic, Sarah explained. And he wrote a lot of the group's songs and kept journals where he jotted down his thoughts and impressions of things that had happened to him, and ideas for songs and song titles, plus he played half a dozen different instruments and he loved to draw.

"And this is all of them?" Grandma was strolling around, studying the magazine covers and pull-out posters Sarah had tacked to her walls. She was looking at a full group shot now, of Zac, Ike, and Tay singing together. "They look very nice. And this one —"

"That's Taylor again," Sarah told her.

"You like him the best?"

"Grandma Lily, it's more than that. Promise you won't laugh at me."

"Never," her grandmother promised.

"I love him," Sarah said softly. "I know that when we meet, something magical will happen. He'll see me. He'll sing just to me. Our souls will connect." She looked away. "You think I'm weird, right?"

Her grandmother smoothed back a loose

strand of Sarah's hair. "I think you're wonderful," she said. "I think you're smart and good and so pretty. Why wouldn't someone special see you and sing just to you? No, I don't think you're crazy, Sarah, not one little bit."

Before she went to bed, Sarah pledged to stay positive. No matter what happened, she would see Taylor.

Even if she and Jennifer didn't get tickets to Hanson's shows, she could still go to the stadium and wait for him to come out. She would make sure he saw her. And when he did, it would be just like the song — *incredible*.

It was still dark when she got up. The sound of a car pulling into her driveway had awakened her. Its beams washed over her bedroom wall, casting a pale glow over the poster of Taylor above her dresser.

Sarah went to the window and looked outside. The car in her driveway was a taxicab, and someone was getting into it.

Before she fell back to sleep, Sarah glanced at the clock. It was midnight.

By morning, she'd almost forgotten the strange incident. When she did remember it, while she was brushing her teeth, it seemed more like a dream than reality.

And so did the positive attitude she'd vowed to keep. She had gotten up feeling seriously grumpy.

She dragged into the kitchen, still in her T-shirt and boxers, her short, dark hair all sleep-tangled. "I don't want cereal," she announced before she even reached the table.

"How about a muffin?" her mother asked, oblivious to Sarah's evil mood.

"Oh, sure. No fat, no-sugar, no taste, my favorite kind," Sarah grumbled. "I'll have toast."

Jeremy came crashing in. "I'll take a muffin," he said. "Blueberry."

"Corn or bran," their mother said.

"Without sugar," Sarah emphasized.

"Yuck." Jeremy switched on the countertop TV. "I want Cocoa Puffs, okay? And chocolate milk."

"In your dreams," Sarah told him as the local news came on. The weather guy was droning about highs, lows, and fronts. "And all you Hanson fans will be glad to know that the weekend looks fine," he announced abruptly. "Not a cloud in sight for that big concert over at Wellburn Stadium."

"Oh, joy," Sarah muttered sarcastically. But she felt a wave of unbearable sadness. Something inside her wanted to cry.

Not that her mother noticed. She just whacked another orange in two, stabbing it just like she had Sarah's hopes.

"Thanks, Tim." The regular anchorman was on the screen now. "And speaking of Hanson, let's go over to East Point," he said, "where fans of the platinum pop group have been lining up all night. What's happening out there, Lisa?"

Sarah's mother turned on the juicer just then, totally drowning out the TV. The screen was full of static for a second. Then it cleared, and they were showing all these kids in beach chairs and sleeping bags and wrapped in blankets, camping outside the Sound Shack, waiting to buy tickets.

There were hundreds of them, thousands. Even if Sarah gulped down her toast and called Jennifer this minute, by the time they got downtown, there wouldn't be a single ticket left.

The juicer was making a terrible racket. Because obviously her mother cared more about nutrition than happiness, Sarah couldn't hear what the reporter was saying now. But the camera was panning toward the front of this incredibly long line that practically wrapped around the block.

There were mostly kids waiting, and some twenty-somethings, and a handful of older people who were obviously buying tickets for their children. There was even a woman with gray hair sitting and reading the newspaper on a white plastic chair just like the ones stacked up in Sarah's garage. She was right up near the front of the line . . . wearing pants and sandals and . . .

"Mom!" Sarah screamed. "Shut it off! Come over here! Look. It's Grandma Lily! Look quick!"

"You're mental," Jeremy said.

"No, seriously," Sarah yelled. "Mom, I think it was Grandma. Is she here?"

"No," Sarah's mother said, all straight-faced and serious. Then she broke into a gigantic smile. "She wanted to surprise you. I think she'll be pretty disappointed that you saw her on television. She was so excited."

Sarah jumped up and hugged her mother. "This is so the best. I can't believe it," she screamed, jumping up and down. "You knew. You knew! How could you not tell me?"

Jennifer hadn't seen the news, so Sarah got to tell her about it at school. They both shrieked and screamed and started to cry. Kids passed them in the hall and stared at them as though they were crazy.

"We're getting Hanson tickets!" Jennifer hollered to Drew, one of their friends, who rushed over and wanted to know what was happening.

"Shut up," Drew gasped. "For real?" And she started to shriek, too.

"You're absolutely sure she was at the front of the line?" Jennifer was clutching the front of Sarah's blouse and tugging at it as she leaped around ecstatically.

"Yes! Totally," Sarah assured her. "She couldn't

have been more than four or five people away from the door."

"Oh, no! What are we going to wear?" Jennifer demanded, releasing Sarah suddenly.

"Well, not this top," Sarah said, trying to smooth the fabric her manic bud had squeezed into a knot of wrinkles.

"They're getting tickets to the concert," Drew was explaining to everyone who passed.

"What, to Hanson?!" came the responses. "That is so def. I'm, like, dying. I'm totally jealous. I love Taylor! How cool is that?"

Grandma Lily had gotten two front row seats for the first night. "It's what you wanted, isn't it?" she asked as Sarah carefully took the tickets out of the envelope and stared at them, awestruck.

"More than anything," she said, and then she started laughing because "More Than Anything" was the name of a song on Hanson's very first album. "Oh, thank you, thank you, thank you, Grandma!"

Her grandmother laughed, too. "It was fun," she said. "And look how happy you are."

She was. Unbelievably happy. Right up until the night of the concert.

"You're not going," her mother said.

"You can't be serious?" Sarah was stunned.

"Not dressed like that, you're not." Her mother

stood at the bottom of the stairs, staring up at Sarah. Her arms were crossed in front of her, in the don't-even-try-it position.

"But, Mom, this is the choicest outfit I've ever had. I didn't go one cent over my clothing allowance. And besides, Jennifer's mother is going to be here to pick me up in like two minutes."

Her father stuck his head out into the hallway.

"Look at her," said her mother. "That dress is too short, the neckline's too low, the heels are too high."

Her father stared up at her. "Wow," he said. Then, "What's wrong with your skin?"

"It's glitter makeup," Sarah explained. "Oh, please don't do this to me now."

"Glitter, huh?" Her father shook his head. Then he put his arm around Sarah's mother's shoulder, and Sarah knew he was going to soften Mom up. "She's not a baby anymore, is she?" he said.

"She's *my* baby," her mother insisted.

"What do you call that color?" her father asked.

"Blue," Sarah groaned.

"Royal blue," her mother said.

Grandma Lily came out of the living room to join the jury.

"Midnight blue," she decided.

Her father nodded. "I like it."

Her mother glared at him.

"The color. I meant the color. But the neckline's too low. Your mother's right, Sarah."

"She could wear a little sweater over it," her grandmother suggested.

"Oh, great. Like what, a turtleneck?" Sarah couldn't believe this was happening.

"I've got something in my suitcase that might be perfect," Grandma Lily said, disappearing back into the living room.

"Mom, I can't wear something of Grandma's to the concert." Sarah rushed down the stairs and pleaded with her mother, "Oh, please don't do this to me."

The doorbell rang. It was Jennifer. She looked awesome in her hot pink crop top and ankle-length floral skirt. Plus she was wearing a floppy hat trimmed with Hanson buttons.

"Jennifer's wearing a long dress," her mother pointed out.

"But her stomach's bare," said her father.

Jennifer looked from one of them to the other, then turned with a questioning gaze to Sarah.

"They want me to wear my grandmother's sweater to Hanson," Sarah explained, mortified.

"We've got to go," Jennifer said. "Just take it, wear it, whatever it is," she whispered. "Even if it's squirrel fur. Let's go. You can always lose it later."

But when Grandma Lily returned, she was

carrying this tiny, sequin-trimmed sweater that was practically a clone of the designer beaded cashmere that Sarah and Jennifer had drooled over on their shopping expedition.

"Oh, that is so cute!" Jennifer gushed. "It totally sparkles."

Sarah hugged her grandmother then slipped into the sweater and whirled for her parents. "Better? Okay? Can I go now?"

Her mother nodded reluctantly.

"You look adorable," her father said, then added reassuringly, "in a grown-up kind of way, of course."

"Go." Grandma Lily patted her back. "Have fun."

How could she not? They were sitting front and center, right down on the floor of the stadium, only a dozen feet from the immense platform where Taylor would perform. All around them, kids were laughing and calling out to one another, squealing and waving signs with love messages for their favorite Hanson. The noise was intense, and the show hadn't even begun yet.

Jennifer was all excited and squirmy. She was turned around, kneeling on her seat, looking for people they knew and, occasionally, shouting in Sarah's ear that she'd spotted someone from school.

But Sarah stared, entranced, at the stage.

There were a dozen people moving around up there, stepping over cables and tinkering with lights or sound equipment, but none of them were Hanson.

Suddenly, the noise in the stadium grew thunderous. The laughter gave way to piercing screams. The shouting became more shrill. It was almost scary, like being inside the whirling funnel of a tornado. Then, as if someone had thrown a switch, the stage was blindingly lit. Laser beams of color sliced the air. Impossible as it seemed, the audience uproar got even louder . . . as Hanson dashed up the steps to the platform, waving and laughing.

Taylor was the first to spring onto the stage.

Tears sprang into Sarah's eyes the moment she saw him.

He was a thousand times more awesome than he'd looked in videos and photographs. He was real.

Then Ike ran on, waving, and then little Zac bolted behind his drum set. The noise and excitement in the stadium drowned out nearly their entire first song.

The show was amazing. The boys sang everything, their platinum oldies and classic new songs from their upcoming CD.

Then Ike played the first chords of "I Will Come To You." The crowd went wild yet again.

Jennifer screamed and bounced up and down in her seat. Wrapped in Grandma Lily's stunning, sparkling sweater, Sarah shivered and hugged herself.

Taylor stepped to the edge of the stage. He grabbed a mike and tossed back his long, gleaming blond hair.

And it happened, just as Sarah had known it would.

Their eyes met. They connected. Sarah felt it like a volt of electricity. And she knew that Taylor had felt it, too.

Looking right at her, he sang "I Will Come To You." He sang as if it were not just a song, but a pledge.

"Jennifer, it happened," Sarah trilled when the concert was over.

"It was so cool," Jennifer gleefully agreed. "We did it. We were in the front row of the most awesome Hanson show ever!"

"He sang to me," Sarah said, grabbing Jennifer's hand and starting to pull her toward the nearest exit. "We've got to get outside and meet him."

"Yeah, I know. He sang to me, too," Jennifer said, rushing alongside her.

"No, I mean, really. He really saw me, Jen. He sang 'I Will Come To You,' staring straight at me the whole time," Sarah explained.

Jennifer blinked at her. "With twenty thousand screaming fans, Taylor actually saw you? I don't think so," she crooned.

"You'll see," Sarah said confidently. "Let's run around to the stage entrance and catch them as they come out."

It was a great idea. So great that only about a thousand other kids had it, too.

It took Sarah and Jennifer fifteen minutes to push, beg, and wheedle their way to the front of the crowd waiting at the team entrance to the arena.

It took another hour and a half to realize that Hanson had left by another exit.

Security guards began to break up the disappointed crowd, shooing everyone away from the stadium. "They're gone. They left over an hour ago. They're probably at the hotel in bed by now, which is where most of you should be."

Sarah couldn't believe it. She was crushed.

"We're locking up now," a guard told her. "You've got to move on. There's another show tomorrow."

"It was totally amazing. You just cannot even imagine," Jennifer babbled when they finally hooked up with her waiting parents.

Jennifer was right, Sarah realized on the ride home. It *had* been a phenomenal evening. And now she had to let go of her disappointment, and get herself psyched up for when she walked into her house. Grandma Lily had been so wonderful. After all she'd done, Sarah wasn't going to hurt her feelings by acting ungrateful or gloomy.

The next day, she did her Saturday morning chores in a fog. *How could it have happened?* Sarah kept wondering. She'd been so sure that she and Taylor had been fated to meet. Could she have been wrong about his singing to her, too?

"Why don't you go for a walk?" her grandmother suggested, removing from Sarah's soapy grasp the egg-scorched skillet she'd been mindlessly scrubbing. "You look pale. Go outside, get some air." Buzzing Grandma Lily's cheek, Sarah dried her hands, grabbed her fleece jacket, and left. She didn't know when the idea occurred to her, or even if it had been an actual idea. She just found herself heading, with a strange determination, toward the stadium.

No one would be there, she knew. Hanson's show was hours away. But something made her keep going. *Maybe,* she thought as she entered the stadium grounds, *I just want to be where Taylor had been.*

Sarah found a quiet bench under a tree, near one of the side doors. For a moment, it was last night again. She was back there, sitting in the front row, watching Tay leap to the front of the stage, coming right toward her. She remembered how the crowd screamed out his name as he grabbed the microphone. She could hear the opening chords of "I Will Come . . ."

Actually, Sarah realized with a start, someone *was* playing the opening chords of the song. There was music coming from the arena.

The side door opened. Sarah was about to ask whoever was coming out what was happening inside. She got as far as, "Excuse me, do you know . . . ?" Then she froze.

It was Taylor. She was staring into Taylor Hanson's baby blue eyes.

"Hey," he said, smiling at her, unleashing the legendary dimple in his right cheek.

"Hi," Sarah stammered, and it happened. It happened again. Taylor's eyes locked on hers.

"I know you," he said slowly.

"I was at the show last night," she told him.

Taylor laughed and flipped back his hair. "Right! You're the glitter girl."

"My name is Sarah," she said, amazed at how easy it was to talk to him. "I was sitting in the front row."

"I know. I saw you when we were doing 'I Will Come To You,'" he said. "You were wearing something that sparkled."

"My grandmother's sweater," Sarah laughed.

"Really? Well, the lights were just glittering off that thing. I couldn't take my eyes off you. I was singing right to you."

"I know," Sarah said. "It was a great concert. I think you're incredible. Totally talented."

Taylor blushed! Sarah was astonished. She cleared her throat. "And your brothers, too, of course," she added tactfully.

"They're right inside." He indicated the side door with a toss of his head. His honey-colored hair swung free, catching the sunlight. "My whole family's there — my sisters Jessica, Avery, and baby Zo, and my little brother Mackenzie. And, of course, my parents. We're getting ready for tonight's show. Doing a sound check. Would you like to meet them?" Taylor asked.

"Wow. I would love to," Sarah said immediately.

"Cool. Come on." He held his hand out to her.

From the shady bench, Sarah looked up at him. "Taylor," she asked, "why did you come out just now?"

His eyes clicked onto hers again. Electricity crackled through them. "To meet you, I guess," he said.

Sarah met and held his smiling gaze. "I knew that," she said, taking his hand and following him into the stadium.

The Hansons were wonderful. While Taylor and his brothers worked with the sound and lighting technicians, his parents, Walker and Diana, put Sarah totally at ease. They asked her a million questions about her family, and told her about theirs. How, because of Walker's job with an oil drilling company, they'd lived all over Latin America, in Venezuela, Ecuador, and Trinidad and Tobago. And Sarah told them about Grandma Lily, and how she'd gone downtown in the dead of night, to wait in line for Hanson tickets.

Which was why, that night, while Sarah watched the concert — *from backstage!* — sitting with Mr. and Mrs. Hanson, and Jessica, Avery, little Mackenzie, and baby Zoe, her entire family sat in the VIP section of the stadium, being totally dazzled by their first Hanson show.

Sarah peeked out at them from backstage. Her little brother, Jeremy, was in ecstasy. He was kidding around with the girl sitting next to him, who was bouncing an I LOVE ZAC! sign. Her mom and dad were holding hands. Her father looked pretty cool in his crewneck sweater and Levi's. And, this was a family first, her mom was wearing jeans, too! But the wonder on Grandma's Lily's face, the utter delight as she looked around at the screaming, cheering Hanson fans, thrilled Sarah the most.

Just as her mom turned and whispered something to Grandma Lily, the group finished "Where's the Love." The audience went wild again. Jeremy jumped up and started whistling and shouting. Her father covered his ears. Her mother and grandmother broke into delirious laughter.

Sarah had never seen any of them looking so free.

And then it was time for Taylor to sing "I Will Come To You." In his red shirt and dark blue pants — red, his sister Jessica had told Sarah, was Tay's favorite color; blue was his next — Taylor charged toward the edge of the stage just like he'd done at yesterday's concert.

Sarah wondered which lucky girl he would sing to tonight. It didn't matter. She had never been happier. She doubted whether she ever would be. *It was not possible,* Sarah thought.

Until, a moment later, when Taylor turned away from the swooning, screaming audience, and sang his song to her.

WHAT'S YOUR
FANTASY DREAM DATE?
TELL US!

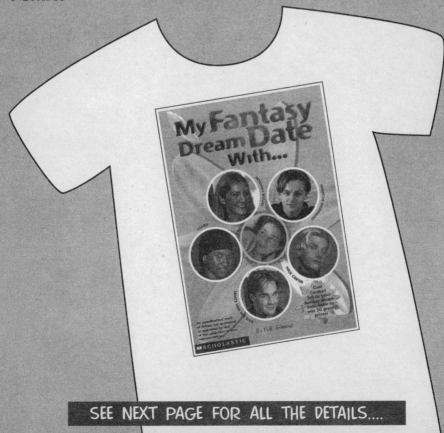

Official Fantasy Dream Date Sweepstakes Rules

1. NO PURCHASE NECESSARY. To enter, complete this official entry coupon or hand print your name, address, age, and telephone number on a 3" x 5" card and mail with your completed fantasy dream date story (no longer than 2 pages, please) to: Fantasy Dream Date Sweepstakes, c/o Scholastic Inc., P.O. Box 7500, Jefferson City, MO 65101.

2. Sweepstakes open to residents of the USA no older than 15 as of 2/1/99, except employees of Scholastic Inc., and its respective affiliates, subsidiaries, and their respective advertising, promotion, and fulfillment agencies, and the immediate families of each. Sweepstakes is void where prohibited by law.

3. Odds of winning depend on total number of entries received. Fifty winners will be randomly drawn by 2/15/99 by Scholastic Inc., whose decision is final. Only one prize per winner. Winners will be notified by mail and will be required to sign and return an affidavit of eligibility and liability release within fourteen days of notification, or the prize will be forfeited and awarded to an alternate winner. Prizes will be awarded by Scholastic upon receipt of affidavit.

4. Prize: A Fantasy Dream Date T-shirt (est. retail value: $25)

5. Prize is non-transferable, not returnable, and cannot be sold or redeemed for cash. No substitutions allowed. All taxes on prize are the sole responsibility of the winner. Except where prohibited, by accepting the prize, winner consents to the use of his/her name, age, entry, and/or likeness by sponsors for publicity purposes without further compensation. By accepting the prize, winner agrees that Scholastic Inc. and its respective officers, directors, agents, and employees will be held harmless against any claims of liability arising directly or indirectly from the prizes awarded.

6. For a list of winners, send a self-addressed stamped envelope to FANTASY DREAM DATE Winners, c/o Scholastic Inc., P.O. Box 7500, Jefferson City, MO 65101, after February 22, 1999.

YES! Enter me in the Fantasy Dream Date Sweepstakes.

Name_____Age_____

Address_____

City_____State_____Zip_____

Phone (_____)_____